BEYOND
ROSWELL

KEN HUDNALL

OMEGA PRESS
EL PASO, TEXAS

BEYOND ROSWELL

COPYRIGHT © 2016 KEN HUDNALL

OMEGA PRESS

An imprint of Omega Communications Group, Inc.

For information contact:

Omega Press

5823 N. Mesa, #839

El Paso, Texas 79912

Or http://www.kenhudnall.com

FIRST EDITION

Printed in the United States of America

**OTHER WORKS BY THE SAME AUTHOR
UNDER THE NAME KEN HUDNALL
FROM OMEGA PRESS
MANHATTAN CONSPIRACY SERIES**
Blood on the Apple
Capitol Crimes
Angel of Death
Confrontation

THE OCCULT CONNECTION
UFOs, Secret Societies and Ancient Gods
The Hidden Race
Flying Saucers
UFOs and the Supernatural
UFOs and Secret Societies
UFOs and Ancient Gods
Evidence of Alien Contact
Intervention
Secrets of Dulce
Unidentified Flying Objects
Sensual Encounters
Strange Creatures From Time and Space
Introduction to Roswell

DARKNESS
When Darkness Falls
Fear The Darkness

SPIRITS OF THE BORDER
(with Connie Wang)
The History and Mystery of El Paso Del Norte
The History and Mystery of Fort Bliss, Texas

(with Sharon Hudnall)

The History and Mystery of the Rio Grande
The history and Mystery of New Mexico
The History and Mystery of the Lone Star State
The History and Mystery of Arizona
The History and Mystery of Tombstone, AZ
The History and Mystery of Colorado
Echoes of the Past
El Paso: A City of Secrets
Tales From The Nightshift
The History and Mystery of Sin City
The History and Mystery of Concordia
The History and Mystery of ASARCO
Military Ghosts
School Spirits
Restless Spirits
Railroad Ghosts
Nautical Ghosts
Haunted Hotels
Haunted Hotels in Arizona and Colorado
Ghosts of Albuquerque

SHADOW WARS
The Shadow Rulers
The Secret Elite

THE ESTATE SALE MURDERS
Dead Man's Diary
A Bloody Afternoon of Fun

Northwood Conspiracy

No Safe Haven; Homeland Insecurity

Where No Car Has Gone Before

Seventy Years and No Losses: The History of the Sun
Bowl

How Not To Get Published

Lost Cities and Hidden Tunnels Along the Border

Vampires, Werewolves and Things That Go Bump In The
Night

Border Escapades of Billy The Kid

Criminal Law for Layman

Understanding Business Law

Death of Innocence: The Life and Death of Vince Foster

PUBLISHED BY PAJA BOOKS
The Occult Connection: Unidentified Flying Objects

DEDICATION

As with all of my books, I could not have completed this book if not for my lovely wife, Sharon.

TABLE OF CONTENTS

INTRODUCTION 9

CHAPTER ONE: ROSWELL 13

CHAPTER TWO: ROSWELL: UPDATE 41

CHAPTER THREE: THE KINGMAN ARIZONA INCIDENT 53

CHAPTER FOUR:THE MEXICAN ROSWELL 73

CHAPTER FIVE: AZTEC - NOT A HOAX 93

CHAPTER SIX: CRASH AT MAGDALENA (HORSE SPRINGS) 111

CHAPTER SEVEN: SAN ANTONIO, NEW MEXICO 123

CHAPTER EIGHT: UFO CRASH AT CAPE GIREADU, MISSOURI 147

CHAPTER NINE: CRASH AT CORONA 154

CHAPTER TEN: THE MEN IN BLACK 155

CHAPTER ELEVEN: UFO RETRIEVAL PROJECT 169

APPENDIX ONE: OTHER CRASHES   203

INDEX   211

INTRODUCTION

A few words about the title. Many people seem to be of the opinion that the crash of a purported unidentified flying object at Roswell was a somehow unique and special occurrence. In fact, the crash of a UFO is not a unique occurrence as there have been several other crashes throughout history. Additionally, it will surprise and shock many people to find out that the UFO crash celebrated at Roswell did not actually take place in or even near the community of Roswell, New Mexico.

The famous crash in 1947 actually occurred near the village of Corona, New Mexico. According to Wikipedia.com Corona is a village in Lincoln County, New Mexico, United States, located on U.S. Route 54. The population was 165 at the 2000 census. Corona was the closest habitation to a purported UFO crash in 1947 about 30 miles (48 km) to the southeast. (See Roswell UFO incident) The rancher who found the crash first came to Corona to report it to a few residents before going to

Roswell to tell officials there about what had crashed on his ranch[1].

Many people who have called into this author's radio talk show[2] seem to be of the opinion that there were actually three UFO crashes in 1947: The Plains of San Agustin, Corona and Roswell. They normally express surprise to find out that the Corona Incident and the Roswell Incident are the same event. Much of the confusion seems to be that Stanton T. Friedman has written about Roswell and also co-wrote a book entitled "Crash At Corona[3]". Unless one reads this material very carefully, you can come away with the idea that he is actually talking about two different crashes. He actually does discuss two separate UFO crashes but the second one is the incident at the Plains of San Agustin, which is a very interesting tale that is not talked about very much.

Of course for every discussed crash, there are an army of doubters who claim that it is al a hoax. Of course, what the supposed hoaxers have to gain is puzzling, but there it is. So this book discusses the major UFO crashes.

---

[1] Wikipedia.com
[2] The Ken Hudnall Show which can be heard by going to http://www.kenhudnall.com and click on the link.
[3] Friedman, Stanton T. and Don Berliner, Crash at Corona, Paragon House, New York, 1992

The dilatants have, unfortunately, taken over the events in Roswell and continue to push their tired old books as if it is somehow something new. So read on and make your own conclusions as to whether or not aliens cashed on earth.

CHAPTER ONE

ROSWELL

While there are millions of individuals who firmly believe in the existence of unidentified flying objects, the consensus of opinion is anything but in agreement regarding what exactly flies our skies. The UFO world is actually a small one, which a few serious researchers and a number of ego driven individuals who care more about enhancing their own reputations than they do about letting the public know what is taking really taking place. For example, there is one who never goes anyplace without his publicist so that everyone knows who he is.

In order to thoroughly understand a subject, a wise researcher wants to study a phenomenon from all sides. In the UFO field, it is necessary to study many encounters and compare both the similarities as well as the differences, not concentrate on just one. However, there are also those who claim to be serious researchers who spend their careers concentrating on just one event, such as the UFO crash at Roswell. Such individuals are merely dilatants, who strut around touting their one or two or three books that purport to be discussions of major discoveries but which are actually just reports of what various people have said to them. Take these so called researchers outside their comfort zone and they attack anything new and different anyone else has to report.

As an example, I wrote a book regarding the untold stories behind many of the alien abductions and because there was a scantily clad young woman on the cover[4], one dilatant[5] decided it was somehow pornographic and demanded it be removed from the Roswell UFO Museum bookstore. Of course he had never read the book, really had no idea what it was about, but he was positive that he knew better than anyone else what the public wanted or needed to see. It is unfortunate that such people are actually listened to by those who should make up their own minds. This was really a ploy to have his own tired old books put more into the public eye as my books have routinely outsold his many times over.

---

[4] Hudnall, Ken, Sensual Alien Encounters, Omega Press, El Paso, Texas (2015)

[5] Who claims to be a leader in the UFO world, but demonstrates a very closed mind to anything he did not write.

This same dilatant was one of those who, in Mexico, to great fanfare, personally identified the mummy of an Indian girl as that of an alien. He was also compensated in an amount far more than he or his opinion was worth. Amazingly, this major misidentification does not seem to have damaged his career though a close examination of the so-called alien figure in question would have revealed the card attached to it properly identifying the Indian girl as a human Native American. But such is the impact that massive egos have on those who are less well informed on the topic in question. It should also be mentioned that it was Albert Einstein who said that condemnation without investigation is the height of ignorance. This describes this dilatant's attitude exactly.

But moving on let us look at what is known about the incident that has become world famous.

The Roswell UFO Crash

Many believe that that the crash happened in or near the town of Roswell. But the unidentified flying object crashed on a ranch northwest of Roswell, New Mexico, sometime during the first week of July 1947. There seems to be no first hand data giving the exact day and time of the

crash.

Figure 1:Many believe a lightning strike brought down the craft at Roswell.

A rancher by the name of W.W. "Mack" Brazel said later he found debris from the crash scatter over a wide area as he and a companion[6], the son of Floyd and Loretta Proctor rode their horses out to check on a flock of sheep after a fierce thunderstorm that had occurred the night before. Brazel said that as they rode along, he began to notice unusual pieces of what seemed to be metal debris scattered over a large area. Upon further inspection, he

---

[6] I have since discovered that there were one or two young Mexican men with Brazel and Proctor that day who were so scared by the ensuing actions of the U.S. Military that they returned to Mexico and refuse to be interviewed about the issue.

said, he saw a shallow trench several hundred feet long had been gouged into the ground by something that had to be fairly large.

Brazel later said he was struck by the unusual properties of the debris and, after dragging large pieces of it to a shed, he took some of it over to show the Proctors. When interviewed, Mrs. Proctor, who later moved from the somewhat remote ranch to a house closer to town, said she remembers Brazel showing up with the strange material and a story of finding it scattered over a large area of the range.

The Proctors told Brazel he might be holding wreckage from an alien spacecraft as there had been a number of UFO sightings reported in the United States that summer. However, he also allowed that it could be wreckage of a government project, as there had been a number of those tested in the New Mexican desert during the war. After some discussion, he decided that he should report the incident to Chaves County Sheriff, George Wilcox.

Figure 2: Chavez County Sheriff Georgie Wilcox

A day or two later, Brazel drove into Roswell, which is the county seat, and reported the incident to Sheriff Wilcox. After examining the pieces of metal that Brazel gave him, Sheriff Wilcox decided this was a matter for the Army and reported it to Maj. Jesse Marcel, intelligence officer for the 509th Bomb Group, stationed at Roswell Army Air Field[7].

Later research revealed that, as in many other cases, shows military radar had been tracking an unidentified flying object in the skies over southern New

---

[77] The U.S. Air Force was not yet in existence. All flying units were under the command of the Army Air Corp. until 16 September, 1947.

Mexico for four days prior to the alleged crash. On the night of July 4, 1947, radar indicated the object had gone down about 30-40 miles northwest of Roswell during a massive thunderstorm. There was later speculation that perhaps the craft had been struck by lightning which had caused the crash.

Another individual came forward later and claimed to be an eyewitness to the crash. This witness, by the name of William Woody, lived east of Roswell. When he was questioned, he said he remembered being outside with his father the night of July 4, 1947, when he saw a brilliant object plunge to the ground. At the time, neither he nor his father had any idea what the object might be.

It is also interesting to note that even though the area in question was somewhat remote from town, there seemed to have been a fairly large number of witnesses to the event. There have long been reports of archeological students on field exercises that saw the crash and rushed to the site. Shortly after they arrived, it was reported that soldiers arrived and chased everyone away. The debris site reportedly was closed for several days while the wreckage was cleared. When Woody and his father tried to locate the area of the crash they had seen, Woody said they were stopped by military personnel who ordered them out of the area.

Major Marcel, after receiving the call from Wilcox and on subsequent orders from Col. William Blanchard, 509th commanding officer, went to investigate Brazel's report and to see if they could identify the craft that was said to have crashed. Marcel and Capt. Sheridan Cavitt, a senior Counter Intelligence Corps (CIC) agent assigned to the Roswell Army Airfield, followed the rancher to his home place. They spent the night there and Marcel inspected a large piece of debris Brazel had dragged from the pasture to his home.

Monday morning, July 7, Major Marcel got his first look at the debris field. Marcel would remark later that "something ... must have exploded above the ground and fell as the debris covered an extensive area." As Brazel, Cavitt and Marcel inspected the field, Marcel was able to "determine which direction it came from, and which direction it was heading. He later said that the debris were scattered in a pattern ... you could tell where it started out and where it ended by how it was thinned out ..."

According to Marcel, the debris was "strewn over a wide area, I guess maybe three-quarters of a mile long and a few hundred feet wide." Scattered in the debris were small bits of metal that Marcel later subjected to a cigarette lighter to see if it would burn.

Along with the metal, Marcel described finding weightless "I"-beam-like structures that were three-eights inch by one-quarter inch, none of them very long that would neither bend nor break. Some of these "I"-beams had indecipherable characters along the length, in two colors. Marcel also described metal debris the thickness of tinfoil that was indestructible.

After gathering enough debris to fill his staff car, Marcel decided to stop by his home on the way back to the base so he could show his family the unusual debris. He'd never seen anything quite like it.

"I didn't know what we were picking up," he later said. "I still don't know what it was ... It could not have been part of an aircraft, not part of any kind of weather balloon or experimental balloon ... I've seen rockets ... sent up at the White Sands Testing Grounds. It definitely was not part of an aircraft or missile or rocket."

Major Marcel's son, Jesse Jr. had the opportunity examine much of the material that his father brought home. Many years later, under hypnosis conducted by Dr. John Watkins in May 1990, Jesse Marcel Jr. remembered being awakened by his father that night and following him outside to help carry in a large box filled with debris. Once inside, they emptied the contents of the debris onto the kitchen floor.

Jesse Jr. described the lead foil and "I"-beams. Under hypnosis, he recalled the writing on the "I"-beams as "Purple. Strange. Never saw anything like it ... different geometric shapes, leaves and circles." He later designed models of these "I" beams that were made available at the Roswell UFO Museum.

Under questioning, he said the symbols were shiny purple and they were small. There were many separate figures. Under hypnosis Jesse Marcel, Jr. remembered that his father than said that the debris had come from a flying saucer. Jesse Marcel Jr. also remembered that he had asked his father what a flying saucer is. He said that he didn't know what a flying saucer was. His father had replied it was a ship.

Major Marcel reported what he found to Colonel Blanchard, showing him pieces of the wreckage, none of which looked like anything Blanchard had ever seen. According to Major Marcel, neither had ever seen anything like these debris fragments.

Bodies

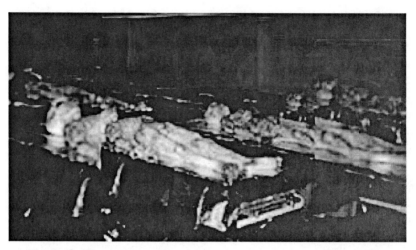

Figure 3: There are many reports of bodies recovered by the U.S. Military

There have long been rumors that bodies of aliens were recovered at the crash site. Several individuals that had come upon the crashed vehicle later reported that they had seen small bodies of what appeared to be dead occupants lying near the craft. However, this has never been confirmed by the military. However, there were a number of witnesses to the presence of alien bodies who seemed to have slipped under the government's radar, so to speak.

Glenn Dennis, a young mortician working at the Ballard Funeral Home in Roswell, received some curious calls one afternoon in July of 1947 from the Roswell Army

Airfield Morgue. According to the phone call, the base's mortuary officer was trying to get hold of some small, child size, hermetically sealed coffins and also wanted to know how to preserve bodies that had been exposed to the elements for a few days and how to avoid contaminating the tissue.

Dennis later said that evening he drove to the base hospital, where he saw large pieces of wreckage with strange engravings on one of the pieces sticking out of the back of a military ambulance. No one seemed to want to discuss what the wreckage had come from. He entered the hospital and was visiting with a nurse he knew when suddenly he was threatened by military police and forced to immediately leave the building.

The next day, Dennis said that he again met with the nurse, who told him about strange looking bodies that were discovered with the wreckage and even drew pictures of them for him on a prescription pad. According to Dennis within a few days she was unexpectedly transferred to England; her whereabouts remain unknown[8]. Steps were

---

[8] Though there have long been questions about the name of the nurse and whether or not she even existed. Dennis did not help matters when he changed her name several times.

being taken to ensure that word did not leak out about the bodies or the crash.

Roswell Army Air Field Press Release

At 11 a.m., July 8, 1947, Lt. Walter Haut, RAAF public information officer, finished a press release Blanchard had ordered him to write, stating that the wreckage of a crashed disk had been recovered and was in the possession of the military. According to a latter statement by Lt. Haut, Colonel Blanchard actually dictated the contents of the famous, or rather infamous, press release about a flying saucer being found by the U.S. Military.

According to the Roswell Daily Record for 8 July 1947 Lieutenant Haut gave copies of the press release to the two radio stations and both of the local newspapers. By 2:26 p.m., the story was on The Associated Press wire:

"The Army Air Forces here today announced a flying disk had been found."

As calls began to pour into the base from all over the world, Lt. Robert Shirkey watched as MPs carried a large amount of material from their carryalls and loaded the wreckage onto a C-54 from the First Transport Unit.

To get a better look, Shirkey stepped around Col. Blanchard, who was irritated with all of the calls coming into the base. Blanchard decided to travel out to the debris field and left instructions that anyone calling him was to be told that he'd gone on leave.

Headquarters Gets Involved

Colonel Blanchard had sent Major Marcel to Fort Worth Army Air Field (later Carswell Air Force Base) to report to Brig. Gen. Roger M. Ramey, commanding officer of the 8th Air Force. Marcel was to brief the General on the UFO situation and also took with him the debris he had collected.

Figure 4: Famous picture of Major Marcel showing wreckage of the purported balloon to General Ramey.

Marcel told Haut years later that he'd taken some of the debris into Ramey's office to show him what had been found. The material was displayed on Ramey's desk for the general to see when he returned from a meeting.

Upon his return, Ramey said that he wanted to see the exact location of the debris field, so he and Marcel went to the map room down the hall, leaving the debris unguarded on the General's desk — but when they returned to the General's Office, the wreckage from the crashed saucer that had been placed on the desk was gone and a weather balloon was spread out on the floor. Maj. Charles A. Cashon took credit for the now-famous photo of Marcel with the weather balloon in Ramey's office however it would seem that this was not the case[9].

It was then reported in the press that there was no UFO as Ramey said that he recognized the remains as part of a weather balloon. Brig. Gen. Thomas DuBose, the chief of staff of the 8th Air Force, later reported that *"[It] was a cover story. The whole balloon part of it. That was the part of the story we were told to give to the public and news and that was it."*

According to the Roswell Daily Record, 9 July 1947, that afternoon Haut's original press release was rescinded and an officer from the base retrieved all of the copies of the press release from the nearby radio stations and newspaper offices. The next day, July 9, a second press release was issued stating that the 509th Bomb Group had mistakenly identified a weather balloon as wreckage of a flying saucer.

On July 9, as reports went out that the crashed object was actually a weather balloon, cleanup crews were busily clearing the debris. Bud Payne, a rancher at Corona, was trying to round up a stray when he was spotted by the military and carried off the Foster ranch. Broadcaster Judd

---

[9] As can be seen in an addendum to this chapter, new information has come to light about this photograph.

Roberts and Walt Whitmore were turned away as they approached the debris field. As the wreckage was brought to the base, it was crated and stored in a hangar. That was very strange handling for something as common as weather balloon wreckage.

Back in town, locals Walt Whitmore and Lyman Strickland saw their friend, Mack Brazel, who was being escorted to the Roswell Daily Record by three military officers. He ignored Whitmore and Strickland, which was not at all like Mack's normal behavior, and once he got to the Roswell Daily Record offices, he changed his story. He now claimed to have found the debris on June 14. Brazel also mentioned that he'd found weather observation devices on two other occasions, but what he found this time was no weather balloon.

Mac Brazel also gave the following interview to the local Roswell Newspaper:

Interview with Mac Brazel - Roswell Daily Chronicle, July 9, 1947

W.W. Brazel, 48, Lincoln county rancher living 30 miles south east of Corona, today told his story of finding what the army at first described as a flying disk, but the publicity which attended his find caused him to add that if he ever found anything short of a bomb he sure wasn't going to say anything about it.

Brazel was brought here late yesterday by W.E. Whitmore, of radio station KGFL, had his picture taken and gave an interview to the Record and Jason Kellahin, sent here from the Albuquerque bureau of the Associated Press to cover the story. The picture he posed for was sent out over the AP telephoto wire sending machine specially set up in the Record office by R. D. Adair, AP wire chief sent here for the sole purpose of getting out the picture and that of sheriff George Wilcox, to whom Brazel originally gave the information of his find.

Brazel related that on June 14 he and 8-year-old son, Vernon were about 7 or 8 miles from the ranch house of the J.B. Foster ranch, which he operates, when they came upon a large area of bright wreckage made up on rubber strips, tinfoil, a rather tough paper and sticks.

At the time Brazel was in a hurry to get his round made and he did not pay much attention to it. But he did remark about what he had seen and on July 4 he, his wife, Vernon, and a daughter Betty, age 14, went back to the spot and gathered up quite a bit of the debris.

The next day he first heard about the flying disks, and he wondered if what he had found might be the remnants of one of these.

Monday he came to town to sell some wool and while here he went to see Sheriff George Wilcox and "whispered kinda confidential like" that he might have found a flying disk.

Wilcox got in touch with the Roswell Army Air Field and Maj. Jesse A. Marcel and a man in plain clothes accompanied him home, where they picked up the rest of the pieces of the "disk" and went to his home to try to reconstruct it.

According to Brazel they simply could not reconstruct it at all. They tried to make a kite out of it, but could not do that and could not find any way to put it back together so that it would fit.

Then Major Marcel brought it to Roswell and that was the last he heard of it until the story broke that he had found a flying disk.

Brazel said that he did not see it fall from the sky and did not see it before it was torn up, so he did not know the size or shape it might have been, but he thought it might have been about as large as a table top. The balloon which held it up, if that was how it worked, must have been about 12 feet long, he felt, measuring the distance by the size of the room in which he sat. The rubber was smoky gray in color and scattered over an area about 200 yards in diameter.

When the debris was gathered up the tinfoil, paper, tape, and sticks made a bundle about three feet long and 7 or 8 inches thick, while the rubber made a bundle about 18 or 20 inches long and about 8 inches thick. In all, he estimated, the entire lot would have weighed maybe five pounds.

There was no sign of any metal in the area which might have been used for an engine and no sign of any propellers of any kind, although at least one paper fin had been glued onto some of the tinfoil.

There were no words to be found anywhere on the instrument, although there were letters on some of the parts. Considerable scotch tape and some tape with flowers printed upon it had been used in the construction.

No strings or wire were to be found but there were some eyelets in the paper to indicate that some sort of attachment may have been used.

Brazel said that he had previously found two weather balloons on the ranch; but that what he found this time did not in any way resemble either of these.

"I am sure what I found was not any weather observation balloon," he said. "But if I find anything else besides a bomb they are going to have a hard time getting me to say anything about it."

It was an interesting about face; clearly the cover-up was working to intimidate the witnesses.

The Las Vegas Review Journal, along with dozens of other newspapers, carried the AP story:

"Reports of flying saucers whizzing through the sky fell off sharply today as the Army and the Navy began a concentrated campaign to stop the rumors."

William Blanchard

Figure 5: Col. William Blanchard

The story also reported that AAF Headquarters in Washington had "delivered a blistering rebuke to officers at Roswell." However, if this true it had little or no effect on the career of Colonel Blanchard. Clearly, Colonel Blanchard was following the orders he received on how to handle the recovery of this mysterious craft. Had he been acting on his own, his military record would not have been as stellar as it was later seen to be.

In fact, Colonel William "Butch" Blanchard was, according to many of the Roswell books, a key player behind the scenes in the recovery of the Roswell disk and in the development of the cover-up conspiracy that many maintain still exists today. If anyone was to be punished for the story, Blanchard would be the obvious person to feel the wrath of the Department of Defense as he was the one

Figure 6: Major Jesse Marcel

that personally authorized the press release to be sent out. In fact, in the August/September 1992 issue of **Air & Space/Smithsonian Magazine**, Frank Kuznik wrote:

"*Before my trip to Wright-Patterson, I tracked down Walter Haut, the retired base public information officer who wrote the infamous press release, and asked him if he ever actually saw the wreckage. 'No, and I feel like an idiot every time somebody asks me that,' he said ruefully. 'I got a call from the base commander, who basically dictated what was in the press release.'"*

If the Department of Defense was angry at the participants in the flying saucer incident, why was no one's career damaged? A West Point graduate, Blanchard rose rapidly through the ranks during World War II, and by 1947 was considered a rising star in the Army Air Corp/Air Force. Such a fiasco as Roswell should have derailed his career, but rather than any permanent damage, by 1966, he was a 4-star general, Vice Chief of Staff, and a "sure bet" to be appointed to serve on the Joint Chiefs. Unfortunately, he died from a massive heart attack at his desk at the Pentagon, cutting short his illustrious career. However, you must ask yourself if the press release that Blanchard dictated to Lieutenant Haut was a major error on his part, how is it that the Colonel went on to become a 4-star general. Screw ups do not get one promoted then or now.

Despite his many later achievements in the Air Force, Blanchard is best known today as the Commanding Officer of the 509th Bomber wing and Roswell AAFB during the Roswell Incident.

The Roswell Incident first became public when the now famous Press Release was sent out by RAAFB Public Information Officer Lt. Walter Haut on July 8, 1947. It is widely believed by many UFO researchers that Col. Blanchard had been ordered by the Pentagon to issue the news released as part of a carefully calculated plan to cover up the recovery of a real extraterrestrial spaceship and its alien crew. The news of a "captured Flying Disk" prompted many reporters to try and contact Col Blanchard for comments, but all they got from his office, during the afternoon of July 8th, was that "no further details were available".

By late afternoon of July 8, callers to the office of Col Blanchard were told that he had "left on leave"!! Roswell proponents have long claimed that this leave was just a ruse to get Blanchard out of the limelight while he commanded the effort to complete the recovery efforts and send the debris and bodies to more secure areas. This claim is based on surmise, and the comments from some (but not all!) of The Witnesses interviewed by researchers.

Another key player in the Roswell saga was Major Jesse Marcel. If he was one of those that was reprimanded for the flying saucer story his career did not suffer for it. Having served as an officer in the Army for a number of years, I am here to tell you if you screw up to the point that Generals have to get involved to correct the issue, your career suffers and suffers big time. However, let us look at Major Jesse Marcel.

Jesse Antoine Marcel was born May 27, 1907 to Theodule and Adelaide Marcel in Terrebonne Parrish, Louisiana. He apparently spent his whole youth there, as he graduated from Terrebonne High School.

After high school, he worked as a draftsman for the Louisiana Dept. of Transportation, the US Army Corps of Engineers, then for the Shell Oil Company as a cartographer, specializing in making maps from aerial photography. Along the way, he served two three-year enlistments in the National Guard—In Louisiana from 1925 through 1928 then in Texas from 1936 through 1939.

He and his family (wife and one son, Jesse A. Marcel Jr.) were living in Houston TX when WWII broke out, and in March 1942 at the age of 35, he applied for and was given a commission as a 2nd Lieutenant in the U.S. Army Air Force. Based on his experience in mapping and analyzing aerial photography, the Army sent him off to Harrisburg, PA for training as a Combat Photo Interpreter/ Intelligence Officer.

Jesse did well in intelligence school—well enough that his next assignment was to be an instructor at this school. Eventually the Army granted his request for combat, and in October of 1943, 1st Lieutenant Marcel found himself assigned to the 5th Bomber Command in the southwest Pacific Theater. For the next two years, Marcel fought the war, first as a Squadron Intelligence Officer then Group Intelligence Officer, participating in several campaigns that resulted in the retaking of the Philippines Islands.

During his combat tour, Jesse performed his duties well. His commanders rewarded his work and abilities with two Air Medals, the Bronze Star, a promotion to Captain, and then to Major in May, 1945. Just before the dropping of the Atomic Bomb, Major Marcel was sent back to the States to get training in the use of Airborne Terrain Mapping Radar systems.

With the war over, Marcel was reassigned in January, 1946 to the 509th Composite Group at the Roswell Army Air Force Base (The 509th later became the 509th Bombing Group and then, with the separation of the Army Air Corp as the U.S. Air Force, the 509th Bombing Wing.) In July 1947, Marcel briefly found himself the center of attention when he brought in the debris of a "Flying Disk" that Mac Brazel had found on Foster's Ranch. At this point, he should have been forced to resign, transferred to a backwater assignment as a result of the flying disk story.

However, in August 1948, he was transferred to the Strategic Air Command, where he was eventually put in charge of a Pentagon briefing room for the Air Force Office of Atomic Energy (AFOAT-1). There his responsibilities were to make sure that materials (charts, illustrations, etc.) were produced and ready on schedule, and to maintain the organization of the briefing room staff. If he was punished for his part in the Roswell UFO story, his career certainly did not show it.

Figure 7: Brigadier General Thomas Dubose

In January 1949, he signed a statement that he fully intended to continue his career in the Air Force, but in the following year he received word that his elderly mother required assistance that his sister could not provide. His request for a hardship release from active duty was granted, so in July 1950 he returned to Houma, Louisiana. There, he drew on his long time hobby in Ham Radio to become an Electronic Repairman, specializing in Televisions, Transmitters and Receivers. When he was released from active duty, his commission (as a Lieutenant Colonel – clearly he was not blacklisted as he was promoted) was transferred to the Air Force Reserves, and he eventually received his full discharge in 1958. Jesse Marcel died in 1986 at the age of 79.

Jesse, in spite of his claim that he was under orders to never, ever talk about his role in the alien disk recovery, occasionally did let on to others that that he had been once involved in a UFO recovery. In 1978, one of his Ham Radio correspondents mentioned Jesse's story to Stanton Friedman, a UFO researcher and a true gentleman, and this led to telling his story of the Flying Disk to the world[10].

As to whether or not there was a government over-up, no less an authority than Brigadier General Thomas Dubose signed an affidavit on September, 2001 which confirmed that there was a cover up. In the affidavit he stated *"After the plane from Roswell arrived with the material, I asked the base commander to personally transport it in a B-26 to Major General McMullen in Washington D.C. The entire operation was conducted*

---

[10] The Roswell Files

under the strictest secrecy. The weather balloon explanation for the material was a cover story to divert the attention of the press[11]."

So while there are a number of questions still to be answered about Roswell and there seems to be little question about the fact that a crash did take place, however, this does not mean that Roswell is the only crash site of a UFO in the world or even in the United States. Actually there have been several crashes of unidentified flying objects in the southwest region that have all been called either hoaxes or misidentifications. Apparently, the military would have everyone believe that a civilian cannot identify a crash flying saucer.

It is interesting to note that the military has tried to convince the news media from that day forward that the object found near Roswell was nothing more than a weather balloon. However, the evidence and numerous witness statements do not support this premise.

---

[11] Affidavit of Brigadier General Thomas Dubose

CHAPTER TWO

ROSWELL: UPDATE

There has been a great deal of information come to

Figure 8: The famous Ramey photo.

light over the years regarding Roswell and the aftermath. There are actual witnesses who have never come forward due to being terrified at the warning given them by the U.S. Military. I know of two who admit that they were there working for Brazel, but they absolutely refuse to discuss it.

However, I was recently made privy to some information about the photos taken of Major Marcel and General Ramey that I am going to share.

This is the famous photo taken of General Ramey inspecting the wreckage. As can be expected, these initial photographs taken of some of the Roswell debris have caused a bit of confusion about the whole incident. Various conflicting statements about these photos have sent researchers running in numerous directions.

Some of the principal people involved in taking these photos are still alive. One of the most interesting individuals is J. Bond Johnson, one of the civilian

Figure 9: Irving Newton was brought in by General Ramey and was ordered to identify the debris as parts of a weather balloon for the benefit of the press corp.

photographers.

According to his story on the afternoon of Tuesday July 8, 1947, Bond Johnson, then a young reporter for the Fort-Worth Star Telegram was told to go out to General Ramey's office with his camera and take some pictures. When he got to the general's office, he said that he saw the floor covered with debris of some kind. Johnson used a Speed-Graphic camera and took a total of eight photographs on the two-sided film plates.

Johnson stated that the debris was pretty plain looking and not very exotic, which led many critics to claim that it could not possibly have come from a high tech, space-traveling vehicle. However, it must be remembered that the Mars Rover and Lunar Lander are pretty ordinary looking also. If one of them crashed they would also look like a pile of ordinary junk.

Bond Johnson, who later became Colonel Bond Johnson and served four tours of duty at the U.S. Pentagon, has stated clearly that the debris he photographed were not pieces of a weather balloon. He also remembers that the debris filled the room with a strong, burned smell. In fact, everyone who entered Ramey's office on that memorable day remembered the strong odor from the debris. Bond says the photos he took were of the real debris received from

New Mexico. If there was a switch of the real wreckage for pieces of a weather balloon, the switch took place after he left.

Ibn the 1990s, almost fifty years after he took those photos, Johnson decided to go back and look at the original photographic plates, which he still had access too. He had not seen the plates since that fateful day of July 8, 1947 when he developed those photos. He was also the last civilian to ever see the Roswell crashed flying-saucer debris[12].

Johnson left his home in Southern California and went down to the University of Texas at Arlington where the original plates had been stored. With special permission, Johnson was able to examine the original plates and have photographic copies made from them. Inexplicably, one of the original plates was missing and no one knew where it was. This missing plate has raised some interesting questions regarding what many believe to be a continuing cover-up.

When Johnson returned to California, he invited MUFON investigators Ron Regehr and Debbie Stock to examine the photos he had brought back. After a thorough

---

[12] Assuming what he saw was actually the real debris.

study, these two investigators made an amazing discovery that had been completely overlooked by everyone for over fifty years. One of the photos clearly shows General Roger Ramey kneeling next to the debris with a piece of paper in his hand. Enlarging the photo allowed the three investigators to determine that the piece of paper held by General Ramey was actually a telegram and with careful enlargement, they were actually able to read parts of the telegram!

To ensure that there were no errors, Johnson, Regehr, and Stock hired six separate teams of experts to blow up and examine the telegram in Ramey's hand. All six teams pretty much concluded the same thing.

THE TELEGRAM

The enlargements clearly reveal that the piece of paper was a Western Union telegram. Besides being able to read the Western Union mark on the telegram, the telegram mentions the "victims" of a second crash site. It also contains the words: "crash story," and "weather balloons." Here are exactly the words that the researchers were able to see on the telegram:

- ...4 HRS THE VICTIMS OF THE...
- YOU FORWARDED TO THE...AT
- FORTWORTH, TEX.
- ...THE "CRASH" "STORY"...FOR 0984
- ACKNOWLEDGES...EMERGENCY
- POWERS ARE NEEDED SITE TWO
- SW MAGDALENA, N MEX.
- ...SAFE TALK...FOR MEANING OF
- STORY AND MISSION...WEATHER
- BALLOONS SENT ON THE...AND
- LAND...ROVER CREWS.

The telegram makes it clear that there was, as many have believed, a second UFO crash at Magdalena, New Mexico. From Ramey's point of view, the fact that there were two crashed discs found in such a short time may have indicated that there was some sort of invasion taking place. It would certainly support the fact that there was a cover-up ordered to give the military time to find out what was taking place.

THE THREATS

I had long heard about the citizens being threatened by the military if they talked about the crash at Roswell, but

I never really understood how serious this became until my short discussion with the two, then boys, witnesses who returned to Mexico to escape what they perceived as a serious threat. Both of these boys help Mac Brazel around his ranch. One of them was the relative of a friend of my wife's. He has never returned to this country as a result of those threats. After some digging I discovered the following information.

Roswell Citizens Threatened

Even though the U.S. Military continued to tell the world that nothing had happened at Roswell, over the next several months following the crash, military personnel and civilians, including women and children, were threatened with death by members of the U.S. military if they spoke of what they saw at Roswell. Many, many civilians have made sworn affidavits stating that U.S. military officers threatened them overtly, boldly, and face to face.

This is very chilling to hear. These threats come a scant two years after the U.S. defeated Hitler in World War II. Even when fighting against Hitler, private citizens and children were not threatened with death if they spoke to a fellow countryman, but here in Roswell, they were! All for a weather balloon? Think again!

While people are certainly capable of making up weird stories, what reason would a mother have for falsely stating that her children were threatened with murder by soldiers from her own country? There were many women who have made such statements about the incident at Roswell.

Even the most hardened police officers will tell you that suspects will say anything and witnesses may be unclear on what they saw, but people who are not involved in criminal activity never make up threats. It just doesn't happen. The following news story is a sample of the stories that came out of Roswell.

Figure 10: Sample news headline

What is interesting is that it was not just ranchers and other residents who were threatened to keep their mouths shut. Even law enforcement officers were told that their lives and their families' lives would be in jeopardy if they talked about the Roswell incident. Military officers made it clear they were willing to murder women and children in retaliation for information being leaked. Does it seem logical that all of this was being done for a mere weather balloon[13]? Some of the reports make it sound like

---

[13] http://www.aliens-everything-you-want-to-know.com/index.html - an interesting website for your review.

the military was using Gestapo tactics to keep the citizens of Roswell under control. What had the military so scared?

Glenn Dennis the young mortician who had been ordered to deliver child size coffin to Roswell Army Air Base and was visiting a friend at the Roswell Army Airfield Hospital when he saw what he believes were two alien bodies reported that two military officers told him that "*If you open your mouth we'll be picking your bones out of the sand.*"

According to Inez Wilcox, the wife of Sheriff George Wilcox, in a discussion with her granddaughter Barbara Dugger, Military Police came to the jail and told both Sheriff Wilcox and his wife that if they ever told anyone anything about the incident that not only would they be killed, but that their entire family would be killed.

According to Frankie Rowe, a child who had seen some of the metal: "*The military came to our house and they basically threatened us if we said anything about it. They were going to take Mother away and they were going to take Daddy away.*"

"*The other guy was standing beside him with his rifle at half-mast, holding it pointed up right in front of their bodies.*"

According to Helen Cahill, sister of Frankie Rowe in a signed affidavit, dated November 22, 1993: "*My sister Frankie told me about her experiences sometime in the early 1960s. Frankie told me about sitting around the table in 1947 and being threatened. My sister also mentioned seeing the material that "ran like water.*"

Frankie Rowe in an affidavit signed November 22, 1993:

"*A few days later, several military personnel visited the house. I was questioned about the piece of metal I had seen. I was told that if I ever talked about it, I could be taken out into the desert never to return, or that my mother and father would be taken to Orchard Park, a former POW camp.*"

According to Roy Danzer, a local plumber who reported that he had seen a still living, but clearly dying alien on a stretch at the Base hospital, Military Officers had also threatened him. He said that they told him that: "*We'll know if you talk; we'll know who you talk to and all you will simply disappear. So forget everything you saw and hightail it out of here before someone else sees you and wants to make sure you stay silent.*"

According to Sally Dwyer, Dan Dwyer's daughter, military personnel told her that *if I didn't forget what my father had told me, that me and the rest of my family would simply disappear in the desert."*

These reports just came from those who were not afraid to talk, so it makes you wonder what threats were used for the ones who have not come forward?

CHAPTER THREE

THE KINGMAN ARIZONA INCIDENT

Figure 11: Location of the Kingman, AZ crash.

"The case of the Kingman UFO retrieval was later brought to the public attention by Raymond Fowler, a respected UFO researcher, in June 1973. It involved an engineer who took preliminary measurements to assess the momentum of a crashing craft, measurements useful to any reverse engineering efforts. The engineer who brought this story to light was Arthur G. Stancil (previously known by the pseudonym "Fritz Werner").

"Stancil graduated from Ohio University in 1949 and was first employed by Air Material Command at Wright-Patterson Air Force Base in Dayton, Ohio as a mechanical engineer on testing Air Force aircraft engines. Dr. Eric Wang who was suspected of leading a reverse engineering team on alien craft headed the Installations Division within the Office of Special Studies where Arthur worked".

"The case of the Kingman UFO retrieval was then brought to the public attention by Raymond Fowler, a respected UFO researcher, in June 1973. It involved an engineer who took preliminary measurements to assess the momentum of a crashing craft, measurements useful to any

Figure 12: Low Boy said to be used to transport crashed UFOs

reverse engineering efforts".

"The engineer who brought this story to light was Arthur G. Stancil (previously known by the pseudonym "Fritz Werner"). Stancil graduated from Ohio University in 1949 and was first employed by Air Material Command at Wright-Patterson Air Force Base in Dayton, Ohio as a mechanical engineer on testing Air Force aircraft engines. Dr. Eric Wang who was suspected of leading a reverse engineering team on alien craft headed the Installations Division within the Office of Special Studies where Arthur worked."

"Stancil signed a legal affidavit vouching to the honesty of his testimony, who has been was released by Ray Fowler in UFO Magazine, April 1976.

"Stancil told that he was loaned out to the Atomic Energy Commission and was designated as a project engineer on some atomic bomb tests referred to as "Operation Upshot Knothole". The location of these tests was at Frenchman's Flats at the southern end of the Nevada Test Site. The test director was a Dr. Ed Doll".

ADDITIONAL INFORMATION:

Stancil worked for Raytheon in Sudbury, Massachusetts in the early seventies on avionics systems. It is unknown as to whether he had further involvement with alien technology, especially since it is likely that he worked for Dr. Wang at some point. Dr. Wang was an Austrian-born graduate of the Vienna Technical Institute, and close associate of Victor Schauberger who had according to the legend developed a concept of a flying disc and allegedly worked on the German flying disc program as early as 1941. Wang taught structural and metallurgical engineering at the University of Cincinnati from 1943 to 1952. Dr. Wang supposedly examined some of the recovered crashed discs and compared them to the vehicles tested in the alleged German V-7 program, but found the retrieved craft to be different in nature.

In 1949, he became Director of the Department of Special Studies at Wright-Patterson where he worked long hours in cooperation with scientists from the Office of Naval Research and with Dr. Vannevar Bush and others from the "Research and Development Board." Dr. Wang relocated his research from Wright-Patterson to Kirtland

AFB in Albuquerque, New Mexico. Dr. Wang passed away on December 4, 1960.

Curiously, Leonard Stringfield, who re-opened the case in his work on UFO crash-retrievals, mentioned testimony he had gotten from a Naval Intelligence Officer who had seen bodies from a crash that occurred in the Arizona desert in 1953. He viewed the bodies at Wright-Patterson when the crates arrived at night aboard a DC-7. There were five crates in all, three of which contained little humanoids about four feet tall. Their heads were hairless and disproportionately large with skin that looked brown under the hangar lights. They were wearing tight-fitting dark suits. It has been suggested by some researchers that these bodies could have come from the crash mentioned by Stancil.

Engineer Bill Uhouse claims there was a crash of an Ebans (Ebens) aerial craft near Kingman, Arizona in 1953 and that four entities survived. That would have been six years after the more famous Roswell crashes and retrievals of "interplanetary craft of unknown origin." In Kingman, according to Uhouse, two disabled Ebens and two more that were in good condition were retrieved by U. S. Government units specially trained for retrieval missions[14].

The two non-humans in good condition were allowed to re-enter the craft and the disabled entities were taken to an unspecified medical facility. He also states that a recovery crew that entered the craft to inspect it came down with a mysterious sickness. The craft was then loaded aboard a trailer and hauled off to the Nevada Test Site north of Las Vegas.

Some implied that Ebans (Ebens) also were a class of EBEs with certain distinct physical characteristics and were said to be working with our military scientists and engineers on various projects. According to BJ, no language interface with the EBE existed in 1953, so a series of symbols were shown to test his reactions. Some symbols looked like letters and others were geometric shapes. The first symbol the EBEN pointed to looked like a "J." The other was an "inertial-bar" that looked like a rod. So, humans called the Eben "J-Rod."

OTHER COMMENTS:

---

[14] More support for the existence of specialized crash retrieval units which would support the existence of a specialized organization that deals with UFOs and aliens.

A researcher adds:

"There were only two seats in the craft. As always there are more questions, but no one to question about these events unless someone else who was a participant steps forward with their testimony."

Indeed, Stancil was a participant and did step forward with an affidavit. The Vietnam commander who told the story in 1964 is an interesting lead. Of course, if additional witness stepped forward, the case would appear even more serious. There are indications of another Arizona UFO crash in 1953, April 18, from which the 3 bodies mentioned in Springfield's story might have come.

A researcher added:

"Strange as it seems it was during the 1950s that various aircraft companies started research projects on the control of gravity and electro-gravitational propulsion. It is possible that these projects constituted some of the first reverse engineering projects on extraterrestrial propulsion systems."

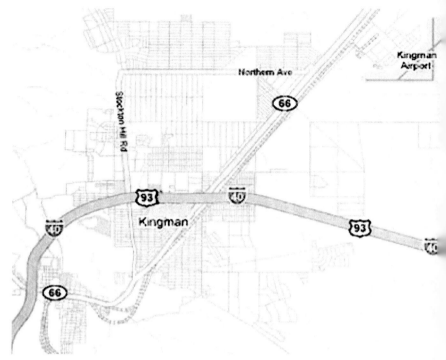

Figure 13: Kingman, Arizona

But we have seen no positive results. Of course Air Intelligence had to try reverse engineering, and maybe promoted such research projects, but it was bound to fail: to understand such advanced flying machine would require a full understanding of the physics, and technology to manufacture the parts. If you had provided the Space Shuttle to Orville and Wilbur Wright, they would have learned nothing useful from it. Unless... you would have explained the physics and provided the technology also. Something to think about.

"Fritz Werner's" Kingman Crash

Below is an account of an alleged flying saucer crash in Arizona reported in a work entitled — Casebook of a UFO Investigator[15]

In 1973 I came even closer to documenting the reality of crashed UFOs, with a signed affidavit from an alleged member of the USAF investigating team! He must remain anonymous; I've dubbed him Fritz Werner.

I, Fritz Werner, do solemnly swear that during a special assignment with the U.S. Air Force, on May 21, 1953, I assisted in the investigation of a crashed unknown object in the vicinity of Kingman, Arizona.

The object was constructed of an unfamiliar metal which resembled brushed aluminum. It had impacted twenty inches into the sand without any sign of structural damage. It was oval and about 30 feet in diameter. An entranceway hatch had been vertically lowered and opened. It was about 3-1/2 feet high and 1-1/2 feet wide. I was able to talk briefly with someone on the team who did

---

[15] Raymond Fowler (Prentice-Hall, 1981, page 199-203)

look inside only briefly. He saw two swivel seats, an oval cabin, and a lot of instruments and displays.

A tent pitched near the object sheltered the dead remains of the only occupant of the craft. It was about 4 feet tall, dark brown complexion and had 2 eyes, 2 nostrils, 2 ears, and a small round mouth. It was clothed in a silvery, metallic suit and wore a skull cap of the same type material. It wore no face covering or helmet.

I certify that the above statement is true by affixing my signature to this document this day of June 7, 1973.

Signature: Fritz Werner
Date Signed: June 7, 1973
Witnessed By: Raymond E. Fowler
Date Signed: June 7, 1973

I watched as Mr. Werner carefully read and signed the final piece of documentation to a 65-page report I had prepared for NICAP. My attempts to substantiate Fritz Werner's incredible story had put me in contact with the AEC, Stanford Research Institute, Wright- Patterson AFB, former Project Bluebook personnel, and a number of persons within the military-industrial complex. Although no additional witnesses could be found, the peripheral names, positions, tests, dates, and places mentioned within

Mr. Werner's personal account all check out exceptionally well.

Mr. Werner had kept his bizarre experience a closely guarded secret for almost exactly twenty years. If true, his story indicates that the physical recovery of manned UFOs had been kept secret for over two decades.

Between June 1949 and January 1960 Fritz held several engineering and management positions at Wright-Patterson AFB near Dayton, Ohio. During the period in which the incident took place, he worked within what was known as the Air Material Command Installations Division, within the Office of Special Studies headed by Dr. Eric Wang. His special ties at that particular time included the engineering design of Air Force engine test cells, development techniques for determining blast effects on buildings and structures, and the designing of aircraft landing gear. Fritz worked his way up to become chief of alighting devices within the aircraft laboratory, Wright Air Development Center; which position led him up to management positions at Wright-Patterson, and later at a variety of civilian companies involved with defense contracts. At the time of his reported experience, he was on special assignment to the AEC at the atomic proving ground in Nevada.

STATEMENT OF FRITZ WERNER

I was project engineer on an Air Force contract with the Atomic Energy Commission for "Operation Upshot-Knothole." My job involved the measuring of blast effects on various types of buildings especially erected for the tests.

On May 20, 1953, I worked most of the day at Frenchman Flat. In the evening, I received a phone call from the test director, Dr. Ed Doll, informing me that I was to go on a special job the next day. On the following day, around 4:30 P.M., I reported for special duty and was driven to Indian Springs Air Force Base near the proving ground where I joined about fifteen other specialists.

We were told to leave all valuables in the custody of the military police. I gave them my wallet, watch, pen and other things I don't remember. We were then put on a military airplane and flown to Phoenix. We were not allowed to fraternize.

There, we were put on a bus with other personnel who were already there. The bus windows were all blacked out, so that we couldn't see where we were going. We rode for an estimated four hours. I think we were in the area of

Kingman, Arizona, which is northwest of Phoenix and not too far from the Atomic Proving Ground in Nevada. During the bus trip, we were told by an Air Force full- Colonel, that a super-secret Air Force Vehicle had crashed and that since we were all specialists in certain fields, we were to investigate the crash in terms of our own specialty and nothing more.

Finally, the bus stopped and we disembarked one at a time as our names were called, and escorted by military police to the area that we were to inspect. Two spotlights were centered on the crashed object, which was ringed with guards. The lights were so bright that it was impossible to see the surrounding area. The object was oval and looked like two deep saucers, one inverted upon the other. It was about thirty feet in diameter with convex surfaces, top and bottom. These surfaces were about twenty feet in diameter. Part of the object had sunk into the ground. It was constructed of a dull silver metal like brushed aluminum. The metal was darker where the saucer "lips" formed a rim, around which were what looked like slots. A curved open hatch door was located on the leading end and was vertically lowered. There was a light coming from inside, but it could have been installed by the Air Force.

My particular job was to determine from the angle and the depth of impact into the sand, how fast the vehicle's forward and vertical velocities were at the time of impact. The impact had forced the vehicle approximately twenty inches into the sand. There was no landing gear. There also were no marks or dents that I can remember, on the surface—not even scratches. Questions asked, having nothing to do with our own special areas, were not answered.

An armed military policeman guarded a tent pitched nearby. I managed to glance inside at one point and saw the dead body of a four foot human-like creature in a silver metallic-looking suit. The skin on its face was dark brown. This may have been caused by exposure to our atmosphere. It had a metallic skullcap device on its head.

As soon as each person finished his task, he was interviewed over a tape recorder and escorted back to the bus. On the way, I managed to talk briefly with someone else who told me that he had glanced inside the object and saw two swivel-like seats as well as instruments and displays. An airman, noticing us talking together, separated us and warned us not to talk with each other.

After we all returned to the bus, the Air Force Colonel in charge had us raise our right hands and take an oath not to reveal what we had experienced. I was instructed to write my report in longhand and not to type or reproduce it. A telephone number was given me to call when the report was complete. I called the number and an airman picked up the report. I had never met nor talked with any of the investigating party. They were not known to me, although I think I recognized two officers' faces. One was from Griffiss Air Force Base at Rome, New York, and the other was involved with an Air Force Special Weapons Group based at Albuquerque. I later saw and recognized the Colonel-in-charge in a movie concerning Project Bluebook.

Mr. Werner confided that a year after his experience he was assigned to serve Bluebook as an official consultant. He sympathized with the Air Force's secret handling of the UFO problem: It did not have an answer regarding where UFOs originated. He felt that they probably still don't know. He said, however, that the Air Force did believe that UFOs were interplanetary vehicles and did not want to create national panic. In response to my questions relating to UFO propulsion systems, he said:

"Well, we all had our guesses as to what it was. At the time, I happened to have contact with a professor in Germany from a very famous university. The Air Force had a contract with them to study antigravity. We didn't call it that exactly, but that's what the popular term was in which you would use the earth's magnetic fields as a form of propulsion. They were able to–with a lot of power, by the way–produce an antigravity machine. It was very impractical and as far as I know, still is impractical, but someday it will be perfected.'

Fritz Werner's credentials are impressive. I checked out his professional resume by calling former employers during a careful character check. Neither of the two former Bluebook officials that I talked with would confirm the incident. One asked, "Where is the object now?" The other got very nervous when I mentioned Dr. Eric Wang's Office of Special Studies. He asked me to leave him alone, as he wanted to live out his life in privacy.

The AEC in Washington and in Nevada both confirmed the dates and names of the tests that Fritz mentioned. They also confirmed the name of the test director, Dr. Ed Doll, and the chief of the Office of Special Studies as the technical and scientific monitor for the project. Further investigation revealed that Dr. Wang had died. I did manage to track Dr. Doll to Stanford Research Institute, but their personnel department did not know his whereabouts. They felt he had died.

Through correspondence with the Mohave County historian I found that Kingman was an unlikely place for the incident to have occurred. A four-hour drive at night in a bus with blacked-out windows could have conveyed the investigating team to any number of places. The historian felt that the vast range controlled by Luke AFB, southwest of Phoenix, was a more likely spot for the crash site. He stated that it is a real desert area with packed sand just as Fritz Werner described.

There were some inconsistencies associated with Fritz's story, but most appeared to be memory lapses. Former employers and professional acquaintances held Mr. Warner in high esteem. Everyone described him as a highly competent, technical, and moral individual. I found that he holds two bachelor's degrees, in mathematics and physics, and a masters degree in engineering. He is also a member of a number of professional organizations such as the American Association for the Advancement of Science, and is involved in a variety of civic groups. The only out-of-the ordinary activities in his personal record are a keen interest in parapsychology, and past involvement–with other professional people–in psychic experiments. In my final report, I discussed the possible explanations of his account. There seemed to be no motive for a hoax, and no apparent evidence for a psychosis. His associates felt strongly that he was not the type to perpetrate practical jokes.

To pin down the exact date of the crash, Fritz mentioned that he may have written something in his diary at that time. After a search, he found the penciled diary that he kept meticulously in those days. When I examined its pages, there was no doubt as to its authenticity. The obviously aged page for May 20, 1953, read:
"

Spent most of the day on Frenchman's Flat surveying cubicles and supervising welding of plate girder bridge sensor which cracked after last shot. Drank brew in eve. Read. Got funny call from Dr. Doll about 1000. I'm to go on a special job tomorrow.
My eyes then skipped over to the entry on May 21.

"Up at 7:00. Worked most of day on Frenchman with cubicles. Letter from Bet. She's feeling better now– thank goodness. Got picked up at Indian Springs AFB for a job I can't write or talk about. [italics mine]

Tantalizing as the Werner story might be, we still have no proof that such incidents have occurred. (How many would believe the government were it to state that studies had been made of crashed UFO vehicles and occupants? Some still believe our manned trips to the moon were simulated in Hollywood studios.)

CHAPTER FOUR

THE MEXICAN ROSWELL

A/K/A

THE COYAME AFFAIR

While there has been much fanfare about the incident in Roswell, it is far from being the only incident of its kind, though most were not received with as much fanfare as in Roswell. In 1974 there was another event that resulted in the crash of a private plane and the crash of what was purported to be a UFO just south of El Paso, Texas. The incident referred to as the Mexican Roswell took place about forty miles south of the Texas/Mexican Border. This event is also referred to as the Coyame, Mexico UFO Crash.

It involved the mid-Air Collision between a UFO and a Small Airplane. Some conspiracy theorists believe the UFO was retrieved by a United States rapid response team assembled by military and intelligence agencies.

Coyame is in the desert of Chihuahua and is also the same desert that surrounds Roswell New Mexico and is about 40 miles (64.373 kilometers) from Texas borders[16].

On Sunday, August 25, 1974, U.S. Air Defense radar at the United States Naval Air Station in Corpus Christi, Texas picked up an object that was, at first, assumed to be a meteor. The object was 200 miles out in the Gulf of Mexico heading for Corpus Christi. The radar operators were baffled as their instruments showed that the object was reaching speeds of 2,500 miles per hour and flying at an altitude of 75,000 feet. At that period in time, jet aircraft could barely reach 2,200 miles per hour and rarely flew above 50,000 feet. After being alerted by the Corpus Christi Naval Air Station, other radar sites began to monitor the strange visitor, among them the Long Range Radar installation at Ellington Air Force Base near Houston, Texas, Lackland Air Force Base at San Antonio, Texas and the FAA radar facility at Oilton, Texas.

There was some initial concern that it might be a ballistic missile, as well as the question of who it got to within 200 miles of the US coast without being seen. However, there seemed to be little excitement until the

---

[16] Noe, Torres and Ruben Uriarte, <u>Mexico's Roswell: The Chihuahua UFO Crash</u>, RoswellBooks.com, 2nd Edition (May 1, 2008)

object being tracked made a thirty-five-degree change in course that alerted the United States Air Force that the object being tracked was not a meteor or a ballistic missile; an air defense alert was called but before any form of interception could be scrambled, the object turned and flew into Mexican territory out of United States air space[17].

Within twenty minutes of crossing into Mexican air space,

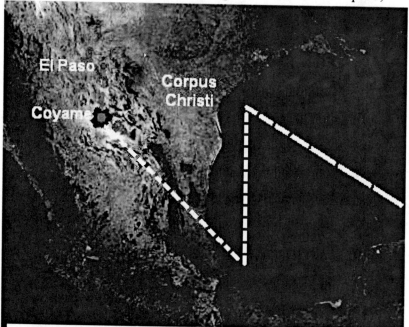

Figure 14: Course flown by the mystery object tracked by radar

the mysterious object disappeared from the radar. Fifty-two minutes after the disappearance of the unknown object, civilian radio traffic indicated that a civilian aircraft had

[17] Noe, Torres and Ruben Uriarte, The Coyame Incident: UFO Crash Near Presidio, Texas, RoswellBooks.com, 2013

gone down in that same area where the mystery object has disappeared from radar.

Figure 15: Location of the Zone of Silence

In trying to piece together what happened, it is clear that at approximately 10:10 PM, the radar image veered to the west and entered Mexican air space about forty miles south of Brownsville, descending from 75,000 feet to approximately 45,000 feet as it reached landfall. AS it flew further inland, it began to descend in stages. At a speed of 2,000 miles per hour, the visitor to earth's skies flew north-west, crossing the Mexican states of Tamaulipas, Nuevo Leon, Coahuila and Chihuahua, seeming avoiding major population areas and military installations[18]. It did come very close to the famous La Zona del Silencio or the Zone of Silence which has been the scene for a number of very bizarre sightings and UFO encounters.

---

[18] Ibid

The Mysterious Zone of Silence

Before we move on it is important that the reader understand exactly what the Zone of Silence actually is. *La Zona Del Silencio*, or the *Zone of Silence*, is a patch of desert near the Bolson de Mapimi in Mexico, in a place known as the Trino Vertex.

The first reported incident related to the Zone of Silence occurred in the 1930's when a pilot by the name of Francisco Sarabia was flying over the area and claimed his instruments went wild and his radio stopped working. Later, in the 1970's, a great deal of attention was drawn to the area when a faulty American missile was fired from the White Sands Missile Base in New Mexico. The missile went off course and crashed, some say was pulled—into the region. The Mexican government allowed U.S. Air Force officials to investigate the crash at the site, which is when the strangeness of the area became apparent. It was discovered that no signals of any sort are able to penetrate the area—including radio and satellite signals—due to local magnetic fields that create a dark zone, thus attributing to the popular name of the site.

Research has since been done at the site, and the Mexican government has even constructed a research complex said to be studying the unusual local habitat and wildlife. Theorists speculate the government is studying more than it is admitting, and there are plenty of anomalies to research in the Zone. One of the many unusual observable properties in this area is its high levels of magnetite and uranium deposits, to which scientists attribute electromagnetic pulses that are said to be the source of the disrupted signals. The area is also a hotbed for meteorites, the remnants of which scientists theorize exude magnetic properties that may explain why so many iron-rich objects from space end up here.

Other, more unexplainable, activity of this nature is reported here, such as the area's reputation for strange lights, UFO sightings and alien encounters. Some even believe it has been used in the past—and present—as a portal for aliens. Ranchers have cited tales of strange lights and odd strangers that appear from nowhere and claim to come "from above". In fact, the same three blonde strangers have often been spotted by multiple witnesses in different areas, but at the same time. Also, the witnesses of some of the unexplainable flying objects—some being described as 'disc-like'—that were thought to have landed in the Zone found physical evidence in the form of burned brush and vegetation at the touchdown sites.

On an interesting note, the Zone of Silence is geographically parallel with the Egyptian pyramids and the Bermuda Triangle, and is located just north of the Tropic of Cancer. Scientists at the Mexican research center have coined the area the Sea of Thetys because it lies at the bottom of what was an ocean millions of years ago. Can any of this explain the numerous strange incidents here?

No concrete evidence has been found to support the claims of extraterrestrial activity in this area, though there are undoubtedly several occurrences that cannot be explained. If the Zone has a rare magnetic pull, one has to speculate the extent of the effect it has on the happenings in the area. Could this area possibly be another Bermuda Triangle of activity? It certainly exhibits much of the same behavior. Add to that the countless testaments of extraterrestrial sightings and this area is certainly a hotbed of activity that requires considerable exploration.

Back To Our Story

The mystery craft was over the northern part of the Zone of Silence when to everyone's surprise, it simply vanished. A number of witnesses to the event believed that the mystery object has just dropped below the radar's horizon. They believed it was still flying, but it was below radar as a result many radar operators believed it was case closed. However, this was not to be the case.

At about 9:30 PM, a Cessna 180 had taken off from the El Paso International Airport. The Cessna, which was of Mexican registry and it passengers, who are still unknown, crossed the international border into Mexico. According to existing records, the Cessna 180 was flying at about 150 miles per

Figure 16: A Cessna 180

hour at an altitude of between 3 and 7,000 feet. At about 200 miles southwest of El Paso, Texas, the plane flew over the mountain range of Northern Mexico and was on a course toward Coyame, Chihuahua, within 50 miles of the Texas border and only a short distance from Presidio, Texas.

The plane's last reported position was about 100 miles northeast of Chihuahua City. About 10:30 PM, the plane suddenly vanished from radar and was presumed to have crashed in the vicinity of Coyame, Chihuahua,

Mexico. Though it was suggested that the missing civilian aircraft might have been the mystery object that had been tracked on radar, additional research made it clear the missing aircraft that had departed El Paso International Air Port to fly to Mexico City could not have been the object being tracked over the Gulf of Mexico. U.S. authorities presumed a collision took place between the civilian aircraft and the mystery object as both disappeared in the same area at the same time.

Based on the monitored radio traffic and satellite feedback and images from covert flyovers, it was believed that the Mexican authorities found the missing plane in a mountainous region near Coyame, Chihuahua, Mexico. Since the crash had been so late at night, the Mexican first responders made no move to reach the crash site until early on the morning of Monday, August 26. Many have tried to trace the path that our aircraft took to aid in reaching the purported crash sight. Since it is known that the U.S. Helicopters that recovered the crash disk entered Mexican airspace just north of Candelaria, Texas, most believe that the recovery sight was in the desert just to the west of Candelaria and just north of Coyame.

The Mexican authorities knew that a plane had crashed enroute from El Paso, but it is not likely that they knew about the crashed UFO. It was not until 8:00 AM that the Mexican rescue efforts began. A spotter plane circled the mountains around Coyame looking for evidence of the wreckage. The spotter plane probably came from one of the two major bases of the Fuerza Aerea Mexicana[19] located in Chihuahua City. Then there were a number of reports that a second plane was on the ground a few miles from the first. Subsequent reports stated the second plane was circular shaped and apparently in one piece although that was visible damage.

U.S. Intelligence was closely monitoring what was taking place. The El Paso Intelligence Center (EPIC), located at Fort Bliss, Texas since 1974 was assigned to monitor the U.S./Mexico Border and took a lose interest in what was happening outside Coyame. Also keeping an eye on what was happening at the crash site were one or more Keyhole (KH 9) spy satellites.

---

[19] Mexican Air Force

Figure 17: Example of the wreckage of a crashed UFO

At about 10:30 AM, U.S. monitors heard a Mexican pilot report finding the wreckage of a small plane. He described it as almost destroyed. Shortly, the U.S. intelligence listeners heard what they had been waiting for, the Mexican pilot radioed back to his base that he had found a second downed "plane" just a few miles from the wreckage. He described this second plane as being nearly intact and circular in shape with a silver metallic finish.

This report resulted in the U.S. Military intensifying its intelligence activity and shifting assets for what might be an incursion into Mexico to take possession of the craft.

Soon after that decline of assistance, the Mexican military clamped a radio silence on all search efforts and any contacts to them were met with responses that ranged from initial claims of ignorance of any crash to eventual total refusal of any cooperation. The CIA and possibly as many as two additional government agencies immediately began forming a recovery team with all required military support, to take the disc by force if it became necessary. In fact, CIA personnel were at Fort Bliss within a short period of time busily putting together a response team. However, it must be noted that the speed this special team and its equipment were assembled suggests that this was either a well-rehearsed exercise or that such an interdiction into foreign countries after purported crashed UFOs had been done before. There have long been reports that the U.S. Intelligence Agencies maintain rapid-deploy recovery teams "sitting on go" for quick missions such as the Coyame crash retrieval[20].

Shortly after the report that there was a crashed UFO not far from the crash site of the small plane, a military convoy left the Mexican Army Base at Ojinga located about 60 miles from the crash site. Reports reveal that the convoy consisted of approximately 24 soldiers and a number of vehicles, to include a large flatbed.

---

[20] Noe, Torres and Ruben Uriarte, Mexico's Roswell: The Chihuahua UFO Crash, RoswellBooks.com, 2nd Edition (May 1, 2008)

There were reports that claimed that at this point, our military offered to come help the Mexican first responders retrieve both aircraft, but the Mexican authorities declined the offer. It was also reported that there was communication held at the highest level, but the Mexican authorities were adamant that they wanted no US involvement.

One reason for U.S. involvement was said to be the fact that the Cessna had left U.S. Airspace. The Mexican authorities were hesitant to allow U.S. involvement and insisted that they knew nothing about a second crashed aircraft. They reported that their operation was just a routine recovery of a crashed aircraft that had nothing to do with the US.

American military scouts were sent in under cover of darkness to monitor the activities of the Mexican recovery effort and reported back that the crashed UFO had been loaded onto a low boy for moving to a more secure site. The circular aircraft was being escorted back to the Mexican military base by a large convoy of support vehicles and armed Mexican troops. Apparently, the Mexican military was taking no chances on anything happening to the mysterious craft before they could study it. However, the scouts reported back that something was clearly wrong and that they first responders were in trouble.

According to one report, the UFO had two holes in its hull, which may have released contaminants into the surrounding atmosphere. Whatever may have been the cause, there was no doubt that something was having a detrimental effect on the Mexican convoy. Clearly the Mexican soldiers had not used any protective gear when they handled both the craft as well as the surrounding debris and something about the craft was causing the Mexican soldiers to become ill.

The intelligence personnel watching on their monitors and listening to the reports of the Mexican military taking the UFO out of reach were glum. In spite of the problems that they were experiencing, the Mexican first responders were guarding the craft and making no effort to distance themselves from the mysterious craft.

Then something totally unexpected happened. Satellite photos, monitors and high altitude aircraft fly-over materials that day indicated that the convoy with the disc had stopped on the side of the access road before reaching any inhabited areas or major roads. There was no visible movement and a number of the vehicles had their doors open. These initial reports were followed with ground intelligence that a number of Mexican military personnel lying on the road. The US military recon-intelligence showed no activity in the convoy and in fact there were numerous signs of that a number of the Mexican military were either dead or very ill. The previously heavy radio contact between the Mexican unit manning the convoy and its headquarters had ceased completely.

No wanting to miss another opportunity to obtain the disk, officials at Fort Bliss, Texas authorized their waiting recovery teams to move out. The US recovery team, believed to be 15 in number and said to have been based at a secret airfield near Alpine, Texas, were fully outfitted with Haz-Mat suits before they left on their recovery mission. Flying nape of the earth to avoid Mexican radar, the unit, believed to consist of 4 Bell UH-1 Huey helicopters and one Sikorsky CH-53D, heavy lift Sea

Stallion crossed into Mexican air space, arriving at the site

Figure 18: Sea Stallion Helicopter

of the Mexican convoy at 16:53, 40 miles inside Mexico, and by 17:14 hours the recovered disk was on its way to US territory. The disk was lifted off the low boy attached to a cargo cable on a Sea Stallion helicopter.

Very concerned regarding the possibility of contamination, and having no idea what had killed the Mexican military personnel, before leaving the convoy site, the U.S. military recovery team gathered together the Mexican vehicles and bodies of the Mexican military, the pieces of the civilian light plane involved in the mid-air collision as well as the bodies of the passenger and pilot of the light plane and destroyed all with high explosives. When U.S. military personnel left the area all of the vehicles that comprised the convoy were burning fiercely. It is believed that the team used a MK-54 SADM "Suitcase Nuke to destroy both the trucks and the bodies of the dead Mexican military. Many agree that this would be a logical step to neutralize any lethal biological agents that might have been released from the crashed UFO.

According to a few people who claim to remember the event, the disk shaped craft was taken directly to a secured hangar at Biggs Field at Fort Bliss, Texas and after some initial study was eventually transferred to Wright-Patterson AF Base. Another report claims that the disc was either transferred after that to another unnamed base, or was taken directly to this unknown base directly from a research facility located outside Atlanta, GA. Due to the possibility of contamination, taking the craft to some of the state of the art decontamination facilities under the control of the CDC would have been a safe bet. However, it would also have taken a possible bio-safety hazard into one of the most populated areas in the country.

What happened to the impact metal debris supposed to be analyze as a suspected metal fusion of the plane and the UFO has never been revealed. Still another report is that due to the possibility of contamination, the disk may have been taken to a classified site high in the Davis Mountains, near Alpine, Texas. There have long been rumors about secret airfields in the mountains above Alpine. Interviews with several long-time residents revealed that as kids they had observed many helicopters making regular trips into some of the more remote areas above Alpine.

So complete was the veil of secrecy about this rash that for almost twenty years, not a word leaked out about this crash. What has become known as the Coyame UFO incident first came to light in 1992, when an account of the case was mailed anonymously to a number of UFO researchers in the United States and Europe. The document was titled "*Research Findings on the Chihuahua Disk Crash*" and was addressed "To All Deneb Team Members, From JS."

In Washington D.C., Elaine Douglass, of the UFO group Operation Right to Know, received a copy and forwarded it to Leonard Stringfield, who included it in his 1994 publication, *UFO Crash Retrievals: Search for Proof in a Hall of Mirrors* (Status Report VII).

Acknowledged as the first UFO researcher to give serious credence to reports of crashed UFOs, Stringfield wrote that the Coyame incident was "authoritatively written, using correct military terminology and, of note and unlike a hoax, draws a line between so-called hard evidence and that which is speculative."

After the report surfaced in 1992, the story of the Coyame UFO incident lay dormant until 2005, when producers of the cable television series **UFO Files**, shown on the History Channel, created a show based on the report. The show, called "Mexico's Roswell," was one of several episodes about UFO crashes similar to the 1947 Roswell UFO Incident.

Written by Vincent Kralyevich and Scott Miller, "Mexico's Roswell" first aired on December 12th, 2005, and featured commentary by veteran UFO investigator Ruben Uriarte, the director of the Northern California chapter of the Mutual UFO Network (MUFON). Uriarte had previously investigated UFO cases in Mexico and was MUFON's liaison to Mexico's civilian UFO groups.

A little bit of investigation with people who were at Biggs Field reveal that the secret airfield near Alpine from which the recovery team was dispatched may well have been Marfa Army Airfield (or Presidio County Airport) a World War II training facility. This abandoned airfield located in the high desert of West Texas, about 200 miles (320 km) southeast of El Paso. However, though it is said to be abandoned, all of the runways, taxiways & ramps of this huge airfield still exist. Many of the wartime buildings were sold at auction and moved to Marfa or nearby Alpine, Texas. Slowly the West Texas desert is reclaiming the large airbase, with tall grass being found on the parking apron, and deteriorating concrete evident on the taxiways and runways. The original main entrance road still exists, but is gated and locked. A small brass memorial plaque can be found on the remains of the World War II adobe block entrance to the post. What better place to base a secret UFO recovery team than at an abandoned airfield that is secured, has no visitors but still has fully functional taxiways and runways?

There have long been rumors of small operational units being based at supposedly abandoned military bases across the country. It is interesting to note that the unit that was sent into Mexico was fully equipped to deal with a potential hazardous situation. The existence of this unit is supported by numerous reports of highly classified recovery units attached to the American Military.

CHAPTER FIVE

AZTEC - NOT A HOAX

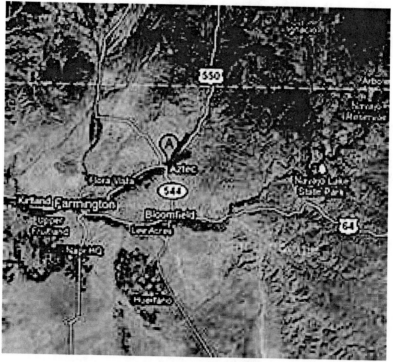

Figure 19: UFO Crash Site at Aztec, New Mexico

Much is made of the 1947 crash at Roswell, New Mexico, but the stories emanating from the town of Aztec, New Mexico of a crash said to have happened there in 1948 are normally written off by most UFO researchers as part of a massive hoax. However, what most UFO researchers seem to have overlooked is that the same man who publicized the crash at Roswell, Stanton Friedman, has studied the research conducted by Scott Ramsey and Suzanne Ramsey and come to the conclusion that a crashed UFO was removed from Aztec and taken away for study[21].

Aztec is a small town near Farmington, New Mexico located in the four corners region of the state. The story of the UFO crash at Aztec actually begins on the night of March 25, 1948. On this particular night, one of the early witnesses, New Mexico police officer Manuel Sandoval spotted one of the familiar glowing disks in the night sky. However, this disk was not exhibiting the usual traits of high speed and agile movements, but rather it was wobbling as if it had trouble staying aloft[22].

---

[21] Ramsey, Scott, Suzanne Ramsey and Frank Thayer, PhD, The Aztec UFO Incident, New Page Books, Wayne, New Jersey (2016)
[22] Ibid

Aztec UFO crash site

Figure 20: Location on Hart Canyon Mesa where the craft is said to have come down.

According to the story told by Officer Sandoval, the UFO was flying very low and slow, barely clearing the canyons as Sandoval pursued the craft toward the Four Corner's area of New Mexico. It appeared to the officer that the UFO was looking for a location so that it could attempt to land. He meant to be there when the UFO touched down.

Valentin Archuleta was a rancher in the area. When he left his home early that morning to begin his daily chores, he said he heard what sounded like a sonic boom. He looked up and saw what he later described as a flying saucer that seemed to be out of control. It was descending toward a mesa across the road from his ranch. He said the flying saucer scrapped the face of the mesa, giving off sparks, but it remained airborne as it headed off in a northerly direction[23]. As the saucer flew out of sight, Valentin headed for the closest telephone which was located at the Blanco Mercantile, a nearby general store. In spite of the very early hour, there was a door that was always unlocked at the store allowing local customers access to the phone[24].

Among the calls that Valentin made were three to Kirtland Air Force Base in Albuquerque, New Mexico[25]. Two of the calls were unsatisfactory, but on the third call, Valentin talked to someone who seemed very interested in his story. The person who answered the phone asked him to repeat his story in some detail as if taking notes. Valentin ask to be called back with information about what the object might be. He never heard anything anyone in the Air Force. However, this does show that the Air Force was aware of the crash even before the craft slammed into the ground.

---

[23] Ibid
[24] Even in 1948, local home telephone service to outlying ranches in areas such as New Mexico was rare.
[25] It should be remembered that the Army Air Corp. became the United States Air Force in late 1947.

Though those who firmly believe that there are no such things as flying saucers were quick to start shooting holes in the Aztec crash story, there are certain pieces of evidence that are visible even today. These items are normally just simply ignored by the debunkers. For example, Valentin reported that the craft scrapped a mesa on his properly before flying off to the north. Even today, anyone who cares to can go to the mesa in question and see the deep marks left in the rocky face of the mesa. However, no one has taken the trouble to thoroughly investigate these marks as it takes permission from the Archuleta family to

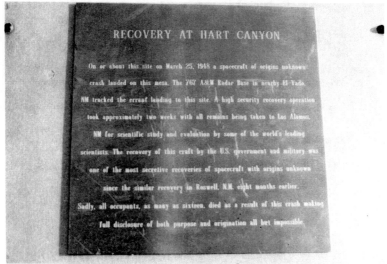

RECOVERY AT HART CANYON

Figure 21: Sign at Aztec, New Mexico

reach the site as it is on their property. So much for a thorough investigation.

There were claims that the mesa was made of sandstone and therefore, there was no way a craft, even if it hit the mesa could have produced the reported sparks. However, a thorough examination of the mesa would show that it was comprised of both sandstone as well as hard volcanic rock[26]. A metal craft hitting the hard volcanic rock would most definitely give off sparks as reported.

Columnist Frank Scully was the first writer to alert and inform the public that a disabled flying saucer had

Figure 22:Downtown Aztec

landed on a mesa 12 miles northeast of Aztec, N.M. Aztec is a small northern New Mexico town near Farmington, best known for its brush with the unknown – the crash of a UFO.

---

[26] Ramsey, Scott and Suzanne Ramsey and Frank Thayer, PhD, The Aztec UFO Incident, New Page Books, Wayne, N.J. (2016)

In his best-selling book *Behind the Flying Saucers* (1950)[27], Scully claimed that a saucer had landed near Aztec on the morning of March 25, 1948 and was observed by locals and oil field workers. (Aztec was an oil town, like Farmington.) Two employees of the El Paso Oil Company, Doug Noland and Bill Ferguson were on their way to the oil fields when they saw the resulting blaze near the oil field drip tanks at the base of Hart Canyon Mesa. Due to the location of the fire in reference to the oil drip tanks, the two decided to go to the fire to determine if it was going to spread in their direction. As a result, these two oil workers were among the first witnesses to get close to the craft. In fact, these two men even climbed on top of the crash UFO and examined it thoroughly.

According to the two men, they found a very large, metallic lens-shaped craft siting silently on top of the mesa. They later described the craft as being brushed aluminum, not the highly polished aluminum like that of an airplane. The skin was very smooth with no noticeable seams, rivets, bolts or weld marks. Doug Noland remarked that it looked almost as if had been molded.

---

[27] Scully, Frank, <u>Behind the Flying Saucers</u>, Henry Holt and Company (1950)

Noland said that he and Ferguson worked their way over the top of the craft looking for an entry point, but found none. They did, however, find what appeared to be portholes. They looked like mirrors until you got very close and then you could see through them. During a later interview, Noland remarked that the portholes looked like the mirrored sunglasses that later became very popular.

Doug Noland also reported that one of the windows or portholes was busted, though he described the hole as being no bigger than a quarter. Looking through the portholes, the two men saw what they described as two small bodies slumped over what appeared to be a control panel of sorts.

According to other witnesses, the craft appeared to be intact except for a fracture in one porthole, was silver in color, circular, and almost 100 ft. in diameter with a dome on top. The cabin feature measured 18' in diameter. The craft lay on the mesa, tilted, due to the hump on the bottom. Later reports placed the number of alien bodies inside the huge craft at sixteen -- all dead[28]. (The body count was later revised to 14.)

---

[28] Ramsey, Scott and Suzanne Ramsey and Frank Thayer, PhD, The Aztec UFO Incident, New Page Books, Wayne, N.J. (2016)

As the two oil workers continued their explorations, other witnesses were arriving. Local ranchers, Mr. and Mrs. Knight ran cattle on the near the mesa and had driven out to make sure that none of their cattle were injured or dead. In later interviews, Noland remembered that the Knights began to lecture the two oil men about getting too close to the craft.

As they discussed the craft and whether or not it was dangerous,

Figure 23: Igor Sikorsky and his new invention

they heard a very strange sound which drew the attention of everyone present. Circling the crash site was a helicopter, something none of them had ever seen before[29]. It is very unusual that a helicopter would be present so quickly after a UFO crash and in such a remote area. Remember this was March of

---

[29] Helicopters was not in general use as of yet. It was very rare to see one outside of a military base at this time. It was never explained how one arrived at Aztec so quickly.

1948 and Igor Sikorsky had only developed the first mass produced helicopter in 1944[30]. Clearly the military was taking the issue of crashed UFO seriously and they were prepared for crash retrievals even in 1948 with the newest technology available to them.

As this was a sparsely settled area, most people who worked and lived in the area knew each other, maybe not by name, but certainly by sight. However, shortly after the Knights arrived, a law enforcement officer from Aztec showed up who was known to a few of the numerous witnesses standing about. He had with him two or three young men who were completely unknown to the many locals witnessing the sight. These young men stood off to the side, never mingled with the other witnesses but kept a sharp eye on both the crowd and the craft. It was suspected by many that they were advance members of the military. The officer from Aztec announced that the military was aware of the crash and that everyone should leave the area. Of course, few, if any, of the locals in the crowd payed any attention to his demand that they leave the area. This was one of the most exciting things to ever happen in the area and they had a front row seat.

---

[30] https://en.wikipedia.org/wiki/Helicopter

According to Doug Noland, the helicopter circled the crash site numerous times before leaving, flying toward the northeast. Ignoring the orders of the police officer to leave the area, Bill Ferguson had gotten a long pole from one of the trucks and was poking around the craft. To everyone's surprise, he activated something and a door or walkway into the craft appeared. Several of the witnesses looked inside to see if there was anyone needing any help. It was reported that the bodies were charred a dark brown and showed no signs of life. Noland remarked that it did not appear that the bodies had a dark skin, but that they had been exposed to tremendous heat. This was a sensational story and one which many sophisticated folks, who were not there, would find impossible to believe.

Military and Scientific Teams arrive

A military security team arrived at the scene in only a few hours, Doug Noland called it late morning and took charge. The members were older and acted as if this (recovering crashed flying saucers) was something that they did routinely. The question on everyone's mind is where did they come from as this was a very desolate part of the country at the time. When questioned later, no one really knew what branch of service these security personnel belonged to as their uniforms were plane and their vehicles were not marked.

The security team took charge in a forceful manner. The onlookers were divided into groups, asked their names, addresses and why they were at that location. Once this information was obtained, the witnesses were sworn to secrecy, and then folks ordered away from the area.

Figure 24: Military security was quickly in place

Hours later, a team of scientists arrived on the scene. They had flown into Durango, Colo., and had been shuttled to the site, probably by auto. After marveling at the uniqueness of the circular craft, they set about gaining entry. Using a pole, they gained entry by widening a cracked porthole, pushing a button or lever, and a door opened on the side of the craft, according to Scully. Most of this is narration, hearsay and undocumented and sounds like science fiction, doesn't it?

Scully reported that he obtained his information from Silas Newton, an oil man and investor, and from a mysterious "Dr. Gee." He further explained that Dr. Gee was really a composite of eight scientists who were at the crash site, some of whom Scully talked with. Dr. Gee was revealed to be an Arizona magnetics engineer who was an associate of one of the eight scientists, but the other names were never revealed.

In a strange turn of events, Scully's story was sought after by a San Francisco journalist by the name of Cahn, who wanted to buy Scully's story. Scully refused to sell and Cahn turned jealous and vowed to "get" Scully.

Cahn reported Scully to the FBI and other government agencies. He wrote an article for True Magazine and labeled Scully's story a hoax.

Cahn also prevailed upon the Denver D.A. to charge Scully with a crime-fraud. A trial ensued and Newton, Scully and "Dr. Gee" (Lee GeBauer) were convicted by a jury. They paid court costs and received no other penalty.

The Federal Government declared the whole case a hoax. The case died, just like Roswell died after the army said the crash at Roswell was a weather balloon. The public, including many UFO researchers, accepted the verdict. It was a hoax, people thought; case closed.

For the record, Newton, GeBauer and Scully maintained for the rest of their lives that they had learned the truth about UFOs and shared it with a public who deserved to know.

UFO Crash at Aztec, A Well Kept Secret

In 1981, an aerospace engineer by the name of William Steinman decided to take a look at the Aztec case. Steinman described himself as a skeptic, but he had read Scully's book and it raised questions in his mind. Did anything really happen in that small town that was covered up by the military?

Steinman went to Aztec, N.M., and began by interviewing locals who knew about the story. At a yard sale he learned where the crash site was. He went there and observed charred rocks and a heavy concrete slab and he noted the remoteness of the site.

He listened and asked questions as locals replayed the story for him.

A UFO had landed or crash-landed at Hart Canyon, was recovered by the military and taken away. The craft was circular, silver in color, 100 ft. in diameter, with a dome on top and bottom. One porthole was fractured. Over a period of three days, the craft was dismantled and hauled at night by large flatbed trucks under tarps to a secure location thought to be Los Alamos. The area was secured by troops for two miles in each direction.

Steinman also reported that the craft had been detected by three radars operating in the Four Corners area. One of these was of a new type and more powerful than the others. One or more of these radars may have interfered with the ship's flight mechanism and caused it to pancake down to the mesa, according to Steinman.

The radar stations notified higher headquarters. A special army unit, the Interplanetary Phenomenon Unit (don't you love that name?), operating out of Camp Hale, Colo., was ordered to the scene. A team of scientists was also assembled and sent to the crash site. The scientists included two of the country's foremost men of science, Dr. Robert Oppenheimer and Dr. Vannevar Bush, according to Steinman.

There is some documentation in Steinman's book for some of these statements. Here is a telex sent from Camp Hale, Colo., to headquarters, Assistant Chief of Staff, G-2 (Army Intelligence), Washington, D.C., at the time of the recovery mission and reproduced on page 45 of Steinman's book:

"FLYING OBJECT OF UNKNOWN ORIGIN RECOVERED NEAR AZTEC, NM. CRAFT APPROX. 100 FEET DIAMETER, 30 FEET HEIGHT, ONE WINDOW, PORT BLOWN, BODIES ON BOARD. ALL OCCUPANTS DEAD, 4 FT. HEIGHT, OVERSIZED HEADS, CRAFT HAS METALIC SKIN THIN AS NEWSPAPER, BUT TWO TOUGH TO PENETRATE BY CONVENTIONAL TOOLS, PRIVATE PROPERTY WAS PURCHASED FROM LOCALS IN ORDER TO FACILITATE TRANSPORTING OF THE CRAFT TO BASE."

There are other documents, exhibits and drawings scattered throughout the Steinman research text relating to more crashed saucers, MJ12 members, medical reports of bodies, Freedom of Information requests, and security considerations. On the whole, good documentation but often hard to read, assimilate, and connect up with the text. This is a research book, not a relaxed read.

The scientist who leaked the whole Aztec crash story to "Dr. Gee" (Leo GeBauer), according to Steinman and Wendelle Stevens (publishers of the book), is named in and pictured in Crash at Aztec. Stevens had also been researching the case.

As readers of The Star Beacon well know, the whole UFO field is complicated and infused with disinformation and secrecy. Much of the story is classified top secret or above and remains classified to this day.

Steinman wrote to another scientist, Dr. Robert I. Sarbacher, who served on various boards and committees with Dr. Bush and other scientists who were believed to have been at the crash site and participated in the recovery. Steinman sought information from Sarbacher by letter and phone about the crash of 1948, 33 years later. Eventually, Sarbacher responded.

The crash was real, he told Steinman, and Drs. Bush, Oppenheimer and John Van Neuman, the country's most famous mathematician and computer designer, were present, he wrote.

Steinman writes that he was thrilled to receive Sarbacher's letter. It was conformation of years of research. The letter is reproduced on pages 324-325 of the text.

Eventually Steinman ran out of time and money. He contacted Wendelle Stevens, veteran UFO researcher (now deceased), who agreed to publish Steinman's research along with his own. This resulted in their privately published book, _UFO Crash at Aztec, A Well Kept Secret_ (1986).

It is well worth a read and study, but I'll save you the trouble. In the book, the Aztec story is related as true, although covered up by the government. However, I must admit that the book is truly fascinating in the amount of detail that is presented.

Steinman ended his first research trip to Aztec by reporting on the large black helicopters that followed him as he pursued his research, and flew over his home in California when he returned there.

CHAPTER SIX

CRASH AT MAGDALENA (HORSE SPRINGS),

Figure 25: Alien Crash

Around the 4th of July every year, Roswell, New

Mexico hosts a UFO festival built around the Roswell

Incident. Months before the event, which is always held the fourth of July weekend, the motels in and around Roswell can be sold out. The festivities normally include a parade, film festival, rock concert, costume contest, bicycle run and a glow-in-the-dark golf tournament. Any spare time the visitor had could be spent at the two UFO museums. Any spare money could be spent for T-shirts, toys, gimmicks and statues that only the outer limits of the imagination can curb. The dilatant gets to strut his stuff and talk about how great a researcher he is and how brilliant his 2 or 3 books are.

(This Chapter quotes several people who reported information. When the word I is used it is not referring to the author.)

But what about the other UFO crash in 1947, the one on the San Agustin Plains? While many talk about the crash at Magdalena, not very many know much about it. Interestingly enough, even among those who know about this crash, there are not very many people who know the details of this particular UFO crash. About the time that the crash occurred at Roswell, New Mexico on July 3, 1947 something most peculiar may have happened somewhere on the San Agustin Plains. There are those who say that something did happen and there are those who say that nothing happened.

Unlike the events at Roswell, the area around Magdalena (also known as Horse Springs) is isolated and due to the isolated location of this crash site, the list of those potentially involved is a short one.

Some of the better known witnesses to this event are:

- Barney Barnett – A long-time resident of Socorro who worked for the Soil Conservation Service. Barnett, who died around 1969, was very well thought of and respected by all who knew him, many of whom are still living in the vicinity. His recollections have never been disproven.

- Harold Baca was a neighbor and friend of Barney Barnett and the father of the proprietor of Harold's Store located on South California Street in Socorro.

- Gerald Anderson was 5 years old in 1947, but has almost-perfect recollection of the happenings in early July, 1947.

- It was reported that there were six archeology students from the University of Pennsylvania doing a dig in the area but they have never been located or identified.

- There were some Army Air Corp (later U.S. Air Force) personnel who became involved. Unfortunately, they were identified only as a disagreeable red-haired officer and a black soldier.

Nothing at all was heard about any of the odd events on the plains for many years. However, around 1967-68 when he was very ill with cancer of the mouth and throat, Barney Barnett told Harold Baca that he believed that his cancer was caused by the flying saucer he saw on the San Agustin Plains.

Apparently not having heard the story before, "Where?" a startled Baca asked Barnett, who replied, "The San Agustin Plains out past Magdalena. There was those little guys and I leaned down to look at them and I got some of that radiation."

It seems that Barney Barnett had not spoken much about his encounter over the years so it was something of a shock to Baca that his friends had never spoken about what had happened to him all those years before.

The Roswell Incident[31], written by Charles Berlitz and William Moore, includes an interesting account of

---

[31] Berlitz, Charles and William Moore, The Roswell Incident,

Barnett's encounter on pages 57 to 63 in which Barnett is supposed to have told several people about it in the 1950s.

According to the Berlitz and Moore, on or about July 3rd, Barnett was out working near Magdalena and he came across "a large metallic object" with some not-exactly-human dead bodies lying around the craft. He described the bodies as having large, round hairless heads with small eyes. Barnett also said that there were others present. He stated that among the small number of people present when he discovered the craft were some archeology students who might have been from the University of Pennsylvania or the University of Michigan. A short time after he found he crashed saucer, all were escorted away by Army Air Corp personnel and cautioned strongly not to say anything about what they saw.

Later Gerald Anderson came forward in 1990 after viewing a segment of "Unsolved Mysteries" telling about the UFO said to have crashed on the San Agustin Plains. Gerald Anderson was 5 years old in 1947 and claims to have been with his father, his uncle, his cousin and his brother on a summer morning when they came across "a silver object stuck in the ground at a weird angle." Later in 1990 Gerald picked out a small hill on Dave Farr's land east of Horse Springs and declared it the place where he and his relatives had found he crashed UFO.

He said that he remembered the archeology students and Barney Barnett and being chased away by the Army Air Corp personnel in the person of a nasty red-haired officer and a black soldier. He also reported that two of the four aliens found around the craft were alive at the time he saw them. Gerald Anderson passed a polygraph test in 1991 but his testimony is understandingly disputed by some UFO experts. To many who style themselves as the leaders in the UFO community if it did not happen at Roswell, it did not happen.

Readers should also note that Barney Barnett makes no mention of the Anderson family's presence, though Anderson stated he remembered Barnett. In the book *Crash at Corona*[32] by Stanton Friedman and Don Berliner, written in 1992, there is a discussion of Anderson's account on pages 89-97 and 105-108.

Stanton Friedman has done some research on the incident at Horse Springs, as have several other UFO experts. But as near as this writer can determine, the

---

[32] Friedman, Stanton T. and Don Berliner, Crash at Corona, Paragon House, New York, 1992.

lengthiest research, as yet unpublished, has been done by Victor Golubic.

Victor, who lives in Phoenix, was one of a number of UFO aficionados that Jacky Barrington, editor of the Magdalena Mountain Mail, referred to various researchers, all for the sake of a story, the big story. All of them were nice but single-minded and multi-worded. Volumes of words on UFOs and aliens bombarded the public in the spring and summer of 1995.

Many serious UFO researchers tend to be mature, but Victor wasn't at all what you would expect. First of all, he was young and although extremely enthusiastic about UFO research, he was able to converse about many different topics. Unlike the authors of a number of books published regarding the Roswell crash, Victor doesn't seem to have a theory into which he bends and crushes the facts to prove he is correct. Like a few of the more serious researchers, Victor would love to find evidence of a UFO crash here but he's equally open to the possibility that it never happened. On July 5th, 1995, he and a friend drove down Route 12 to the place near Horse Springs identified by Gerald Anderson. Victor had already obtained permission from Dave Farr to enter his land. Just north of

Horse Springs, they turned east on a dirt track. Soon they came to a hill on our left and Victor said, "This is it."

It was a hill looking much like every other hill with a few trees. Nothing to say that it was or wasn't witness to something fantastic. The location was surprising because if this were the place, it would be most unlikely for anything to have crashed there without everyone in Horse Springs knowing about it.

Previously, the two had spoken with several people who had resided in the Horse Springs area in 1947 and none remembered anything unusual that summer. Several did remember a plane crash by the Armijo's' old Horse Springs store sometime around 1945. No one could pinpoint the exact year, but one individual interviewed had a distinct memory of going to see the crashed plane. "It was a military plane and the pilot was dead," said one resident of Horse Springs.

That site, which the two examined, yielded nothing, but logically, 50 years wipes away a lot.

The Air Force was a presence in Catron County during the late forties, staffing what they said was a radar tower on the road to the Marvin Ake ranch. People remember seeing Air Force vehicles on the roads, but no one reported seeing one carrying the bodies of the extra-terrestrial kind.

From Quemado to Reserve to Datil and Socorro, in person and by telephone, Victor interviewed people who had lived in these here parts during those years. Infinitely patient, he was willing and eager to spend hours listening to people talk on all subjects. Gradually, Victor would lead them back to the subject at hand. He would return a few months later to talk to them again and telephone at intervals to see if they remembered anything else. With the aid of his computer and out-of-town phone books, Victor tracked down people all over the country.

Tracked them down, talked to them and found nothing really conclusive regarding the San Agustin Plains UFO crash.

"These sources are not named in this unscientific article because we never mentioned any intent to publish our findings; we were just making inquiries. We heard many fascinating tales handed down over the years, but no first-hand knowledge."

A Quemado resident did report meeting a visitor in 1946 (a year earlier than the famous crash) who said, "*I just*

stopped in Magdalena and there was a thing from space.
There's people in it and they tell me one of 'ems still alive."

Another Quemado resident knew a man in Mangus who saw a shiny thing in the mountains one summer in the late forties.

A few Aragon residents recall hearing about the incident. "Just that there was tracks," said one. And from another, "There were strange people. They were moving. It looked like a plate." They admitted that this was hearsay, which they did not necessarily subscribe to.

Most remembered first hearing about the UFO crash in the 1980s when the investigators started appearing in Catron and Socorro counties. There must be people out there who saw or heard something in the fifties or before. But where are they?

After a respectable amount of researcher, there are few answers about this crash, however, there are a great many questions.

- Did Barney Barnett, whose Soil Conservation work usually took him west from Socorro, go east that day and come across the Roswell UFO crash? Could the crash that Barnett saw have been the main part of the crash that also left pieces at Corona?

- Did the crash occur on the San Agustin Plains, but not near Horse Springs? This is the theory I prefer. Remember, Harold Baca quotes Barney Barnett as saying "out past Magdalena." To me that means on the way to Datil but closer to Magdalena. Describing Horse Springs, one would more likely say "south of Datil."

There is some support for an incident at Magdalena, not evidence – but rather hearsay to support this theory. According to a Magdalena resident, the UFO is purported to have crashed about 15 miles west of Magdalena, possibly around Wolf Well or Tres Montanas.

Yet a man from Socorro says Barney Barnett told his father that the crash occurred somewhere between Datil and Horse Springs. Who was telling the truth, both (there may have been two crashes) or neither? Depending on who you believe, this story does have fascinating possibilities.

CHAPTER SEVEN

SAN ANTONIO, NEW MEXICO

San Antonio, New Mexico is a small sleepy New Mexican town located just off of Interstate 25 between Las Cruces and Socorro, New Mexico. It is the home of the world famous Owl Café, purveyors of the best hamburgers in the known world.

There is also a story relating to a UFO crash in San Antonio, New Mexico[33] that dates from 1945. According to

_____

[33] According to Wikipedia.com - San Antonio is an unincorporated community in Socorro County, New Mexico, United States, roughly in the center of the state, on the Rio Grande. The entire population of the county is around 18,000. San Antonio is partly agricultural, and partly a bedroom community for Socorro and White Sands Missile Range. The city supports a few small businesses, which include the original Owl Bar and Cafe (featured on an episode of the Travel Channel's Burger Land in 2013), Manny's Buckhorn Tavern (featured in 2009 on the Food Network's Throwdown! with Bobby Flay, San Antonio Crane, a restaurant featuring Mexican food, a seasonal roadside market, and a general store. San Antonio is the gateway to the Bosque del Apache National Wildlife Refuge. Interstate 25 runs along the west, and U.S. Route 380 begins there and heads east to Carrizozo. The Rio Grande is just to the east of San Antonio, and the BNSF Railway runs through it and has a small yard (not much more than a siding). San Antonio is about 28 miles from Trinity Site, where the first nuclear bomb was

witnesses, in mid to late August 1945 a small contingent of the U.S. Army passed almost unnoticed through San Antonio in mid-to-late August, 1945 on a secret assignment. The military detail apparently came from White Sands Proving Grounds to the east where the bomb was exploded. It was a recovery operation destined for the mesquite and greasewood desert west of Old US-85, at what is now Milepost 139, the San Antonio exit of Interstate 25. Witnesses report that over the course of several days, soldiers in Army fatigues loaded the shattered remains of a flying vehicle onto a huge flatbed truck and hauled it away.

---

detonated on July 16, 1945. Residents reported tremors like an earthquake and the town received some of the remnants of the mushroom cloud (resulting in some radioactive contamination of the area, which faded quickly and does not persist today). The town was the meeting place for the scientists who detonated the bomb.

Figure 26: The Owl Cafe, one of the best restaurants in the southwest

The two witnesses were Remigio Baca[34] and Jose Padilla and they insist that the operation took place between August 20 and August 25, 1945. Padilla, then age 9, and Baca, 7, secretly watched much of the soldiers' recovery work from a nearby ridge. According to their story, they were very interested because they were the actually the first to reach the crash site. What they saw was a long, wide gash in the earth, with a large object lying cockeyed and partially buried at the end of it, surrounding

---

[34] Remigio Baca wrote a book about his story entitled "Born on the Edge of Ground Zero: Living in the Shadow of Area 51. It is now out of print, but went into some detail about what he saw that exciting summer.

by a large field of debris. They believed then, and believe today, that the object was occupied by distinctly non-human life forms which were alive and moving about on their arrival minutes after the crash.

The two boys reported their findings to Jose's father, Faustino Padilla, on whose ranch the craft had crashed. Shortly thereafter, Faustino received a military visitor asking for permission to remove the object from the Padilla's property. The U.S. Army told the public nothing about it, and told the Padilla family it was a "weather balloon," according to Reme and Jose, now in their mid 60s. And the two men insist the Army went to great lengths to keep the operation under wraps, even concocting a cover story to mask their mop-up mission on the ranch.

During their school years, Jose and Remegio, best friends, would sometimes whisper about the events of that August, which occurred before any of the other mysterious UFO incidents in New Mexico, but they didn't talk to others about it on the advice of their parents and a state policeman friend.

The significance of what they saw, however, grew in their eyes over time as tales of UFOs and flying saucers multiplied across the country, especially in a band across central New Mexico. Among the most prominent sightings was Socorro police officer Lonnie Zamora's April 24, 1964 on-duty report of a "manned" UFO just south of Socorro, less than 10 miles north of the heretofore unnoticed 1945 Padilla Ranch crash.

Jose and Remigio were long gone from the area by the time UFOs and flying saucers became news, and although both kept up with Socorro County events, they lost contact and never discussed the emerging phenomenon with each other. Reme moved to Tacoma, Wash., while still in high school and Jose to Rowland Heights, Calif. Then, two years ago, after more than four decades apart, they met by chance on the Internet while tracking their ancestry. It was then their interest in the most intriguing event of their childhood was rekindled.

During one of the conversations, Remigio and Jose decided to tell their story to veteran news reporter Ben Moffett, a classmate at San Antonio Grade School who they knew shared their understanding of the culture and ambience of San Antonio in the forties and fifties, and who was familiar with the terrain, place names, and people.

The following story was written by Ben Moffett and was sent to me several years ago.

SAN ANTONIO, N.M. -- The pungent but pleasing aroma of greasewood was in the air as Jose Padilla, age 9, and friend, Remigio Baca, 7, set out on horseback one August morning in 1945 to find a cow that had wandered off to calf[35].

The scent of the greasewood, more often called creosote bush today, caught their attention as they moved away from this tiny settlement on their horses, Bolé and Dusty. The creosote scent is evident only when it is moist, and its presence on the wind meant rain somewhere nearby.

So, as they worked the draws on the Padilla Ranch, they were mindful of flash flooding which might occur in Walnut Creek, or side arroyos, if there were a major thunderstorm upstream. Gully-washers are not uncommon in late summer in the northern stretches of the Chihuahuan Desert of central New Mexico, especially along the foothills of the Magdalena Mountains looming to the west.

Despite minor perils associated with being away from adults, it was a routine outing for Jose and Reme. It was not odd to see youngsters roam far afield doing chores during the war years. "*I could ride before I could walk,*" said Jose in a recent interview. "*We were expected to do*

---

[35] By Ben Moffett, Mountain Mail, benmoffett@att.net

our share of the work. Hunting down a cow for my dad wasn't a bad job, even in the August heat."

At length, they moved into terrain that seemed too rough for the horses' hooves, and Jose decided to tether them, minus bridles, allowing them to graze. He had spotted a mesquite thicket, a likely place for a wayward cow to give birth, and they set off across a field of jagged rocks and cholla cactus to take a look. As they moved along, grumbling about the thorns, the building thunderheads decided to let go. They took refuge under a ledge above the floodplain, protected somewhat from the lightning strikes that suddenly peppered the area.

The storm quickly passed and as they again moved out, another brilliant light, accompanying by a crunching sound shook the ground around them. It was not at all like thunder. Another experiment at White Sands? No, it seemed too close. "We thought it came from the next canyon, adjacent to Walnut Creek, and as we moved in that direction, we hear a cow in a clump of mesquites," said Reme. Sure enough, it was the Padilla cow, licking a white face calf.

A quick check revealed the calf to be healthy and nursing, and the boys decided to reward themselves with a small lunch Jose had sacked, a tortilla each, washed down with a few swigs from a canteen, and an apple.

As they munched, Jose noticed smoke coming from a draw adjacent to Walnut Creek, a main tributary from the mountains to the Rio Grande.

Ignoring their task at hand, the two boys headed toward it, and what they saw as they topped a rise "stopped us dead in our tracks," Reme remembers. *"There was a gouge in the earth as long as a football field, and a circular object at the end of it."* It was *"barely visible,"* he said, *through a field of smoke.* "It was the color of the old pot my mother was always trying to shine up, a dull metallic color."

They moved closer and found the heat from the wreckage and burning greasewood to be intense. *"You could feel it through the soles of your shoes,"* said Reme. *"It was still humid from the rain, stifling, and it was hard to get close."*

They retreated briefly to talk things over, cool off, sip from the canteen and collect their nerve, worried there might be casualties in the wreckage.

Then they headed back toward the site. That's when things really got eerie. Waiting for the heat to diminish, they began examining the remnants at the periphery of a huge litter field. Reme picked up a piece of thin, shiny material that he says reminded him of "the tin foil in the old olive green Phillip Morris cigarette packs."

"It was folded up and lodged underneath a rock, apparently pinned there during the collision," said Reme. "When I freed it, it unfolded all by itself. I refolded it, and it spread itself out again." Reme put it in his pocket.

Finally, they were able to work their way to within yards of the wreckage, fearing the worst and not quite ready for it. "I had my hand over my face, peeking through my fingers," Reme recalled. "Jose, being older, seemed to be able to handle it better."

As they approached they saw, thought they saw, yes, definitely DID see movement in the main part of the craft.

"Strange looking creatures were moving around inside," said Reme. "They looked under stress. They moved fast, as if they were able to will themselves from one position to another in an instant. They were shadowy and expressionless, but definitely living beings."

Reme wanted no part of whoever, whatever was inside. "Jose wasn't afraid of much, but I told him we should get out of there. I remember we felt concern for the creatures. They seemed like us-children, not dangerous. But we were scared and exhausted. Besides it was getting late."

The boys backtracked, ignoring the cow and calf. It was a little after dusk when they climbed on their horses and dark when they reached the Padilla home.

Faustino Padilla asked about the cow, and got a quick report. "And we found something else," Jose said, and the story poured out, quickly and almost incoherently. "It's kind of hard to explain, but it was long and round, and there was a big gouge in the dirt and there were these hombrecitos (little guys)."

Their tale unfolded as Jose's father listened patiently. "They were running back and forth, looking desperate. They were like children. They didn't have hair," Jose said

"We'll check it out in a day or two," Faustino said, unalarmed and apparently not worried in the least about survivors or medical emergencies. "It must be something the military lost and we shouldn't disturb it. Leave your horse here, Reme, and Jose and I will drive you home, since it's so late."

Two days later at about noon, state policeman Eddie Apodaca, a family friend who had been summons by Faustino, arrived at the Padilla home. Jose and Reme directed Apodaca and Jose's dad toward the crash site in two vehicles, a pick-up and a state police car. When they could drive no further, they parked and hiked to the hillside where the boys had initially spotted the wreckage.

As they topped the ridge, they noted the cow and calf had moved on, probably headed for home pasture, then they walked the short distance to the overlook. For a second time, Jose and Reme are dumbfounded.

The wreckage was nowhere to be seen.

"What could have happened to it?" Reme asked.

"Somebody must have taken it," Jose responded defensively.

Apodaca and Faustino stared intently but unaccusingly at Jose and Reme, trying to understand. They headed down the canyon nonetheless, and suddenly, "as if by magic," in Reme's words, the object reappeared.

"From the top of the hill, it blended into the surroundings," Reme explained recently. "The sun was at a different angle, and the object had dirt and debris over it," which he speculated may have been put there by someone after the crash.

Apodaca and Faustino led the way to the craft, and then climbed inside while Jose and Reme were ordered to stay a short distance away. "I can't see the hombrecitos," Reme offered.

"No," replies Jose. "But look at these marks on the ground, like when you drag a rake over it."

"The huge field of litter had been cleaned up," Reme recalled. "Who did it, and when, I have no idea. Was it the military? Using a helicopter? Or the occupants?"

The main body of the craft, however, remained in place with odd pieces dangling everywhere.

Now it was time for the adults to lecture Reme and Jose, Reme remembers. "Listen carefully. Don't tell anyone about this," Reme quoted Faustino as saying. "Reme, your dad just started working for the government. He doesn't need to know anything about it. It might cause him trouble."

Faustino also worked for the government at Bosque Del Apache National Wildlife Refuge and the ranch itself was on leased federal land. Faustino was a patriotic man and honest to a fault in his dealing with the federal government, according to Jose.

"The government calls them weather balloons," the state policeman chipped in. "I'm here to help Faustino work out the recovery with the government. They'll want this thing back."

"But this isn't like the weather balloons we've seen before," said Reme. "They were little, almost like a kite."

"You're right, Reme. Este es un monstruso, que no Eddie?" Faustino said.

"Yeah, it's big for sure," the state policeman acknowledged.

"And the hombrecitos?" Reme persisted.

"Maybe you just thought you saw them," said Faustino. "Or maybe somebody took them, or they just took off."

Then they headed home. The cow and calf also grazed their way back in a day or two.

Jose and Reme also look back at the incident from the perspective of time. Was the object that required a flatbed truck and an "L" extension a weather balloon, or an alien craft from space or from another dimension?

The two men, now in their mid to late 60s, still have a piece of the craft and know where other parts were buried by the military.

Reme also speculates about how the 1945 incident fits in with the many sightings that were later reported in a ban across central New Mexico and elsewhere, giving rise to a UFO and "flying saucer" phenomenon that is still debated today.

Of course, the story of the UFO Crash in 1945 did not end here. There was a second part to the story, also written by Ben Moffitt[36].

In mid-August, 1945, before the term "flying saucer" was coined, Remigio Baca, age 7, and Jose Padilla, 9, were first on the scene of the crash of a strange object on the Padilla Ranch west of San Antonio, a tiny village on the Rio Grande in central New Mexico.

Both Remigio, or "Reme" as his friends called him, and Jose, believe they saw "shadowy, childlike creatures" in the demolished, oblong, circular craft when they arrived at the scene, well before anyone else.

The U.S. Army told the public nothing about it, and told the Padilla family it was a "weather balloon," according to Reme and Jose, now in their mid-60s. And the two men insist the Army went to great lengths to keep the operation under wraps, even concocting a cover story to mask their mop-up mission on the ranch.

---

[36] New Mexico UFO Crash, Encounter In 1945 Part 2, By Ben Moffett, benmoffett@att.net, Mountain Mail, Copyright© the Mountain Mail, Socorro, N.M., and Ben Moffett, 11-6-3

The recovery operation actually started two days after Reme, Jose, Jose's father, Faustino, and state policeman Eddie Apodaca, a family friend, visited the site on August 18, 1945. It was then that a Latino sergeant named Avila arrived at the Padilla home in San Antonito, a tiny southern extension of San Antonio.

After some small talk, Sgt. Avila got down to business. According to Reme's and Jose's recollection, and what they learned subsequently from Faustino, the conversation went something like this:

"As you may know, there's a weather balloon down on your property," Avila said. "We need to install a metal gate and grade a road to the site to recover it. We'll have to tear down a part of the fence adjoining the cattle guard."

"Why can't you just go through the gate like everybody else?" asked Faustino.

"Well, the problem is that your cattle guard is about 10 feet wide, and our tractor trailer can't begin to get through there," said the sergeant. "We'll compensate you, of course."

The sergeant also asked for a key to the gate until the military could install its own. He also wanted help with security. "Can you make sure nobody goes to the site unless they are authorized. And don't tell anyone why we're here."

"What should I tell them?" Faustino asked.

"You can tell them the equipment is here because the government needs to work a manganese mine west of here," the sergeant said.

"That was to justify the presence of road-building equipment," said Reme in a recent interview. "It wasn't until decades later, on the Internet, that I learned the Army told a lot of fibs along about that time. I found another manganese mine story was used to cover a UFO incident on the west side of the Magdalenas near Datil in 1947, about the time of the Roswell UFO incident."

"I know for sure that the cover story was at least the second piece of misinformation they gave out in a month," noted Reme, a former Marine, chuckling and referencing the acknowledged false press release used to cover the Trinity atom bomb explosion as the first.

It wasn't long after the sergeant's departure that the Army was on the scene with road building equipment. Long before the road was graded, however, soldiers were at the site, carrying scraps of the mangled airship to smaller vehicles that were able to immediately get close to the scene.

Although they were warned by their father to stay away from the area, Jose, sometimes with Reme, and sharing a pair of binoculars, watched from hiding as the military graded a road and soldiers prepared for the flatbed's arrival. Jose actually made off with a piece, which is still in their possession.

"The work detail wasn't too efficient," said Reme, who noted from his experience in the Marines that military parts had numbers and were carefully catalogued. "The soldiers threw some of the pieces down a crevice, so they wouldn't have to carry them," he said. "Then they would kick dirt and rocks and brush over them to cover them up."

According to Jose, four soldiers were stationed at the wreckage at all times, with shift changes every 12 hours. "One stayed at a tent as a guard and listened to the radio. I could hear the music. They'd work for an hour and then lock the gate, climb in their pick-ups and go to the Owl Café, where they'd look for girls. I know because one of my (female) cousins who was there told me."

Once the flatbed was in place, the soldiers used wenches to hoist the intact portion of the wreckage in place. "They had to build an L-shaped frame and tilt it to get it to fit into the tractor-trailer, because it bulged out over one side," Jose said. "They finally cut a hole in the fence at the gate that was 26 feet long to get it out."

Off it went, shrouded under tarps, through San Antonio and presumably to Stallion Site on what is today White Sands Missile Range, where, according to Reme, it still may be today.

Was this clandestine operation undertaken to recover a weather balloon? Or, as Jose and Reme contend, was it something far more mysterious?

"I think the term 'weather balloon' was a euphemism, a catch-all for anything and everything that the government couldn't explain, said, Reme.

Reme and Jose knew about typical military weather balloons. "My father and I found about seven of them before and after the 1945 crash," Jose remembers. "We always gathered them up and gave them back to the military. They were nothing but silky material, aluminum and wood, nothing like what we found in that arroyo in 1945."

"Those weather balloons were not much more than big box kites," said Reme. "They sure couldn't gouge a hole in the ground. Remember, in 1945, despite the bomb, we weren't all that sophisticated. The Trinity Site bomb, Fat Man, was transported on a railroad car to the site. Radar was primitive or non-existent in some places. Maybe the military knew what they had, maybe they didn't, maybe they couldn't say."

Reme and Jose are convinced, and they say Faustino soon came to join in their belief, that the object on the ranch was no mere weather balloon, but an object of mystery. Faustino, however, had no interest in challenging the status quo, nor did state policeman Apodaca, whatever his beliefs were.

And why would a mere sergeant be sent to negotiate with Faustino Padilla on a mission that involved something more than a routine weather balloon flight. "He wore sergeant stripes," Reme said. "That doesn't necessarily mean he was a sergeant. And he was Latino. He was sent to San Antonio because he could communicate with the locals."

Finally, why would the military allow such cavalier treatment of the wreckage, if it were a foreign or alien craft with scientific value?

"I don't know if they knew what they had," Reme said. "It was a fairly crude craft with no parts numbers on it, and the piece we have, we were told is not remarkably machined even for 1945. But there's nothing that says aliens have to travel in remarkable spaceships.

"Given what we know about distances in the universe, space travel seems far-fetched, I'll grant you. Perhaps they got here by some method we can't fathom and they manufactured a crude object here to get around in this atmosphere. We hear about other dimensions, and parallel universes.

"I don't know much about those things. But I do know what I saw, which was some unlikely looking creatures at the crash site. I know that later other people in the area reported similar things. And I know the government was interested in keeping it quiet."

Reme has studied the UFO phenomenon in his spare time over the years, especially as it pertained to New Mexico. "The military opened the door at Roswell, and then they closed it," he said, referring to a July, 1947 report by the Roswell Air Force Base information office about the crash and recovery of a "flying disc" that they reported had been bouncing around the sky. Then the base retreated by reporting it was merely a "radar tracking balloon" that had been recovered.

Details of the Roswell event can be found in a 19-page Freedom of Information Act request by the late New Mexico Congressman Steve Schiff and released by the

General Accounting Office July 28, 1995. It can be found on the Internet at http://www.conspire.com/ds/gao2.html).

The Roswell crash, which along with the sighting of a UFO south of Socorro by city policeman Lonnie Zamora in 1964, are the two most famous of a string of UFO reports over central New Mexico and in all of UFO lore.

From 1946 through 1949, 25 UFO sightings that "may have contained extra-terrestrial life" were reported worldwide by the Center for the Study of Extra-Terrestrial Intelligence. Of those, seven came from New Mexico, including one near Magdalena (1946), Socorro (1947), Roswell (actually near Corona), July 4, 1947, Plains of San Agustin (Catron County), July 5, 1947, Aztec, 1948, White Sands, 1949 and Roswell again, 1949. Another was in the pattern, too, on the Hopi Reservation of Arizona in 1947.

"There was a pattern of sightings and incidents in a ban across New Mexico. Socorro and San Antonio are right at the center," notes Reme. "Our 1945 sighting just adds to that base of information. It's intriguing to say the least. If you were an eyewitness it becomes even more intriguing."

Reme and Jose are excited enough to tell their story after more than 55 years, even knowing the problems that plagued Lonnie Zamora after his spotting a UFO near Socorro, less than 10 miles away, in 1964.

Jose and Reme would like to see an excavation of the crevice where a few odds and ends from their "alien craft" were tossed. The crevice was recently covered up by a bulldozer doing flood control work.

And they'd like to have the part they have from the wreckage examined more closely. They are not eager to surrender it to anyone, however. "I've heard from others that if you give it up to the government, you stand a good chance of not getting it back," Reme said.

A second piece, which Reme likened to the "tin foil in a cigarette pack," is gone. "I used it to stop a leak in a brass pipe under a windmill at our house in San Antonio in the early 50s," he said. "I used it to fill the stripped threads on two pieces of pipe."

Reme said he regrets using it now, but it was handy. "I kept in for years in an old Prince Albert (tobacco) can in the pump house, and it was the nearest thing available." Reme said the foil stopped the leak in the pipe for years. The windmill is now gone and the property is no longer owned by the family.

Finally, Jose and Reme were asked why they decided to tell the tale today, after nearly 60 years.

"It's something you can never get out of your head," said Reme. "When we saw it, we had never heard the term

UFO, and 'flying saucers' didn't become a part of the language until June of 1947 when a pilot named Kenneth Arnold reported nine objects in a formation in the area of Mount Rainier.

"We didn't invent this phenomenon," said Reme. "We experienced it. Others have apparently had similar experiences. I believe Jose and I have an obligation to add our information to the mix."

CHAPTER EIGHT

UFO CRASH AT CAPE GIREADU, MISSOURI

One of the most mysterious stories of a crashed UFO with alien bodies preceded the well- known Roswell event by some six years. This case was first brought to investigators by Leo Stringfield in his book "UFO Crash / Retrievals: The Inner Sanctum."

Charlotte Mann
Granddaughter of Rev. Huffman

He opened a tantalizing account of a military controlled UFO crash retrieval which is still being researched today. The details of the case were sent to him in a letter from one Charlotte Mann, who related her minister-grandfather's deathbed confession of being summoned to pray over alien crash victims outside of Cape Girardeau, Missouri in the spring of 1941.

Reverend William Huffman had been an evangelist for many years, but had taken the resident minister reigns of the Red Star Baptist Church in early 1941. Church records corroborate his employment there during the period in question.

After receiving this call to duty, he was immediately driven the 10-15 mile journey to some woods outside of town. Upon arriving at the scene of the crash, he saw policemen, fire department personnel, FBI agents, and photographers already mulling through the wreckage.

He was soon asked to pray over three dead bodies. As he began to take in the activity around the area, his curiosity was first struck by the sight of the craft itself.

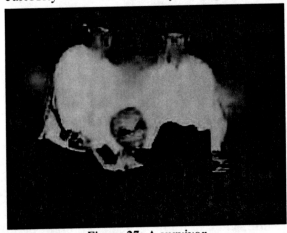

Figure 27: A survivor

Charlotte Mann Expecting a small plane of some type, he was shocked to see that the craft was disc-shaped, and upon looking inside he saw hieroglyphic-like symbols, indecipherable to him.

He then was shown the three victims, not human as expected, but small alien bodies with large eyes, hardly a mouth or ears, and hairless. Immediately after performing his duties, he was sworn to secrecy by military personnel who had taken charge of the crash area. He witnessed these warnings being given to others at the scene also.

As he arrived back at his home at 1530 Main Street, he was still in a state of mild shock, and could not keep his story from his wife Floy, and his sons. This late night family discussion would spawn the story that Charlotte Mann would hear from her grandmother in 1984, as she lay dying of cancer at Charlotte's home while undergoing radiation therapy.

Charlotte was told the story over the span of several days, and although Charlotte had heard bits and pieces of this story before, she now demanded the full details. The secrets of that fateful night were about to be revealed. As her grandmother tolerated her last few days on this Earth, Charlotte knew it was now or never to find out everything she could before this intriguing story was lost with the death of her grandmother.

She also learned that one of the members of her grandfather's congregation, thought to be Garland D. Fronabarger, had given him a photograph taken on the night of the crash. This picture was of one of the dead aliens being held up by two unidentified men.

Charlotte Mann gave, in her own words, an account of what she knew for a television documentary. Some of that account is given here:

"I saw the picture originally from my dad who had gotten it from my grandfather who was a Baptist minister in Cape Girardeau Missouri in the Spring of '41. I saw that [picture] and asked my grandmother at a later time she was at my home fatally ill with cancer so we had a frank discussion.

"She said that grandfather was called out in the spring of 1941 in the evening around 9:00-9:30, that someone had been called out to a plane crash outside of town and would he be willing to go to minister to people there which he did."

"Upon arrival it was a very different situation. It was not a conventional aircraft, as we know it. He

described it as a saucer that was metallic in color, no seams, did not look like anything he had seen. It had been broken open in one portion, and so he could walk up and see that.

"In looking in he saw a small metal chair, gauges and dials and things he had never seen. However, what impressed him most was around the inside there were inscriptions and writings, which he said he did not recognize, but were similar to Egyptian hieroglyphics."

"There were 3 entities, or non-human people, lying on the ground. Two were just outside the saucer, and a third one was further out. His understanding was that perhaps that third one was not dead on impact. There had been mention of a ball of fire, yet there was fire around the crash site, but none of the entities had been burned and so father did pray over them, giving them last rites.

"There were many people there, fire people, photographers, and so they lifted up one, and two men on either side stood him up and they stretched his arms out, they had him up under the armpits and out here.

As I recall from the picture I saw, he was about 4 feet tall, appeared to have no bone structure, soft looking. He had a suit on, or we assume it was a suit, it could have been his skin, and what looked like crinkled, soft aluminum foil. I recall it had very long hands, very long fingers, and I think there were three but I cannot swear to that."

"My grandfather upon arrival, said there were already several people there on the scene, two that he assumed were local photographers, fire people, and so not long after they arrived, military just showed up, surrounded the area, took them off in groups separately, and spoke to each of them.

"Grandfather didn't know what was said to the others, but he was told 'this didn't happen, you didn't see this, this is national security, it is never to be talked about again.'

"My grandfather was an honorable man, being a preacher, that's all that needed to be said to him. And so he came home and told the story to my dad, who was there, and my grandmother and my uncle. Now my mother was expecting at the time, so she was off in the bedroom."

"My sister was born May 3, 1941, so we are assuming this was the middle to the last of April. And he never spoke of it again. But about two weeks later, one of the men who had a personal camera that he had put in his shirt pocket, approached grandfather and said I think someone needs a copy of this.

"I have one and I would like you to keep one. So that's how it came about that grandfather had the picture to begin with. But he never spoke of it again. The other people seem to be very intimidated and very frightened and paranoid."

Other living supporting witnesses include Charlotte Mann's sister who confirmed her story in a notarized sworn affidavit, and the living brother of the Cape Girardeau County sheriff in 1941, Clarence R. Schade. He does remember hearing the account of the crash, yet does not have many details. He does recall hearing of a "spaceship with little people."

Depiction of alien: There are also Fire Department records of the date of the crash. This information does confirm the military swearing department members to secrecy, and also the removal of all evidence from the scene by military personnel.

Guy Huffman, Charlotte's father also told the story of the crash, and had in his possession the photograph of the dead alien. He showed the picture to a photographer friend of his, Walter Wayne Fisk. According to reports, he has been contacted by Stanton Friedman, but would not release any pertinent information.

Charlotte had no luck in getting Fisk to return calls or answer letters. It has been rumored that Fisk was an advisor to the President, and if this was the case, would account for his silence on the facts of the Missouri crash.

This case ends like many others, but appears by all indications to be authentic. All who have come in contact with Charlotte Mann found her to be a trustworthy person who is not given to sensationalism, and has sought no gain from her account.

There is still research being done on the Missouri crash, and hopefully more information will be forthcoming to validate this remarkable case[37].

CHAPTER NINE

CRASH AT CORONA

The crash at Corona was actually the crash made famous by the Roswell Incident. The crash site is actually not too far from the village of Corona, New Mexico. Mac Brazel originally went to Corona to report the crashed UFO, but he was referred to the County sheriff and to find the county Sheriff, he had to go to Roswell, New Mexico.

---

[37] "UFO Crash Retrievals: The Inner Sanctum," by Leo Stringfield.

CHAPTER TEN

THE MEN IN BLACK

Figure 28: Example of Men in Black Sighting

Thanks to the hit movie starring Will Smith and Tommie Lee Jones everybody has heard of the Men in Black (MIBs). The premise of the movie is that the members of this secret group protects the earth from the "scum of the universe." Well, that's just a simple explanation for something a lot harder to explain. The truth is that no one knowns if these guys are government agents, aliens in disguise, or just a group of intelligence operatives trying to keep a secret.

These entities are real. In fact, these mysterious figures have been with us since the early 1940's working to silence witnesses regarding, not just UFOs, but many paranormal events. They generally show up when ordinary citizens have an extraordinary sighting or encounter with a flying saucer or its occupants. They seem bent on intimidating those individuals into not talking about what they have seen. They even attempt to do this with law-enforcement officers and military personnel. There have been hundreds if not thousands of incidents reported about these men in black, though none of the illusive figures have

Figure 29: MIBs seem to inordinately fond of UFO sightings.

ever been apprehended.

Some of these mysterious figures imply that they are working for the government, or the military of specifically the Air Force and this may well be true. However, the majority are certainly not part of any government on this planet. However, there have been reports of so-called Men in Black appearing at events that seemingly have nothing to do with anything related to the government.

GOING BLACK

In the movie, the director of the MIB is shown erasing all governmental files regarding the newly hired member of the Men In Black Organization. First it should be remembered that even though they are called Men In Black, this is not just a reference to their clothing. The word 'black' when used in this context means covert, undercover, not seen. It has been reported that when a person enters the intelligence community and becomes involved in operations and projects, all their government files basically disappear. They are no longer accessible through the normal channels. When this happens it is said the person has "gone black."

However, there is no way that normal intelligent agencies can have the resources to get involved in all of the events where MIBs have been reported. There is something more sinister going on than merely trying to cover up some government project gone astray.

Some people think the MIBs are Aliens

Complicating matters is the fact that many times it appears that the men in black are humanoid-type aliens masquerading as humans. Many people in the military are aware that this may be the case (in some instances).

Alien men In Black?

Are some Men in Black Aliens?

Dr. Herbert Hopkins

Dr. Hopkins was actively investigating a UFO abduction case in 1976 when one evening during the summer a stranger called him on the phone and asked if he could come by and talk to him about the case. This was despite the fact that the case had not been publicized at all. Hopkins agreed, hung up the phone, and immediately walked to his door to turn on the porch light so the caller could see the steps when he arrived. Hopkins was surprised to see a man walking up the stairs of the porch as he was turning on the light. He was shocked when the man introduced himself as the person who had just called him. (There were no cellular phones in 1976.)

The Black Suit Routine

The man was dressed in black suit, black tie, black hat, and gray gloves. In the summertime! The man's skin was a pale sickly color and he appeared to be wearing bright red lipstick, a fact which turned out to be true as Hopkins later watched some of the lipstick rub onto the man's gray glove.

Vanished Into Thin Air

The man asked Hopkins to take out the two coins that were in Hopkins' pocket. Stunned, Hopkins did it. He told Hopkins to watch the coins in his hand. The two coins simply vanished into thin air! Then the man told him, "Neither you nor anyone else on this planet will ever see those coins again." The man then said his "energy was running low" and left. Shortly after stepping off Hopkins' porch, the man himself disappeared.

When the Scare Started

The first widely acknowledged case of Men In Black intimidating UFO witnesses occurred in 1953. A fellow by the name of Albert K. Bender was the editor of a magazine called Space Review. He was also the founder of an organization called the International Flying Saucer Bureau.

During the summer of 1953 Bender apparently discovered some vital information pointing to the cover-up of the existence of flying saucers by the U.S. government. He had written several articles scheduled to appear in the next issue of his magazine. The next thing he knew, three guys show up at his door all dressed in black: black suits, black hats, and sunglasses. They told him they had read his article, even though it had not yet been published. They told him his information was accurate, but that he better not publish the article. In fact, they told him that he'd better not publish anything more about flying saucers. They said, "We advise those engaged in saucer work to please be very cautious." They basically scared him so badly that Bender officially retired from UFO investigations.

Other MIB Reports

* A teenager is threatened by MIBs and has photos of flying saucers seized from him.
* MIBs make a coin disappear from a UFO witness and tell him, "Your heart will do the same if you talk."

* A former Air Force officer who learned about information on extraterrestrials from NASA was harassed, tranquilized, and interrogated.

Even the Military Doesn't Know Who MIB's Are

In 1967 the United States Air Force expressed concern about finding out more about these guys in black who were going around scaring people and saying they were from the U.S. armed services. Here's a statement by Colonel George P. Freeman, the spokesperson for Project Blue Book at the Pentagon:

"Mysterious men dressed in Air Force uniforms or all in black and bearing impressive credentials from government agencies have been silencing UFO witnesses. We have checked a number of these cases, and these men are not connected to the Air Force in any way. We haven't been able to find out anything about these men. By posing as Air Force officers and government agents, they are committing a Federal offense. We would sure like to catch one, unfortunately the trail is always too cold by the time we hear about these cases, but we are still trying."

Assistant Vice Chief of Staff of the United States Air Force Lt. General Hewitt T. Wheless sent a memo on

March 1, 1967 to various agencies in the Department of Defense. Here's what it said:

"Information, not verifiable, has reached Hq. USAF that persons claiming to represent the Air Force or other Defense establishments have contacted citizens who have sighted unidentified flying objects. In one reported case, an individual in civilian clothes, who represented himself as a member of NORAD, demanded and received photos belonging to a private citizen. In another, a person in an Air Force uniform approached local police and other citizens who had sighted a UFO, assembled them in a school room and told them that they did not see what they thought they saw and that they should not talk to anyone about the sighting. All military and civilian personnel and particularly information officers and UFO investigating officers who hear of such reports should immediately notify their local OSI offices."

Some Sample Cases

The following are some encounters with Men in Black that were sent to me by listeners to my radio show[38]. With the secrecy and intimidation still surrounding any

---

[38] The Ken Hudnall Show, heard Monday through Friday from 6-9 PM Mountain Time.

event that has to do with flying saucers or alien beings, people who have these encounters generally don't trust telling someone who doesn't have a clue that these guys even exist.

Larry

Larry was about twenty-five years old, casually but nicely dressed. He reported that: "You know, I had something very strange happen to me and my buddy. I don't like to talk about it because it kind of scares me." So the one who sent the story to me asked him what happened. He was clearly nervous and even stuttered a little. Here's what he said:

Late one night in a state of semi-sleep, he felt a presence in his bedroom. The "presence" communicated with him and let him know it was from another world. Larry asked why all the secrecy and if they were real why they didn't just show up in the daytime. They told him that the next time he was with his best friend (whom they called by name) he would indeed see them and he would know it was them.

Larry said the entire conversation did not exactly take place using words. It was more like he understood what they were thinking and feeling without actual words. I know it sounds weird, but this is very common in human/alien interactions. For the most part, none of the aliens use verbal language, it is all telepathic, and sometimes it's in the human's own language. Many times it is a combination of feeling, "a knowingness", and understanding on a level we have not yet discovered how to describe.

When Larry woke in the morning he wasn't sure if he had been dreaming or not, but the experience was so vivid and unlike any dream he had ever had before that he thought about it daily for months afterwards.

Larry's best friend was now in the military and he didn't see him for months. His friend returned home just in time for the Fourth of July, and they decided to go down to a local park where some of his family members were holding a big picnic. The two of them were just kind of standing around, when a black van pulled up about fifty yards away. The two front doors opened and two men dressed all in black suits with black hats and dark sunglasses got out. Larry was startled because he began to remember his "dream." The two men opened the sliding door on the side of the van and two more guys got out. They too were head-to-toe in black, with shades.

Larry said, "First of all, it was hot. It was the middle of the afternoon and well over 80 degrees, and these guys were in black, with hats! Next, the two guys who got out of the side looked different. They didn't look human. I can't describe it, but their arms looked too long or something. Then they sat down at a picnic table and they all turned around and looked right at me and my buddy. After that he got real quiet. Then they just got back in the van and drove off. My buddy won't talk about it. He pretends like nothing happened, but I know he saw them and he knows I know."

Christine

Christine was career military. She is a pilot and flew in the Armed Forces of the United States. She is even a member of the now infamous "Tail hook Association[39]." Here is what Christine said:

"One night a large UFO showed up and hovered over the base for about forty minutes. Everybody saw it. We were all pilots and we knew it wasn't ours. We could also tell because the brass didn't know what it was either. When

---

[39] For those who don't know, Tail hook is an association for Navy Fighter pilots. The name Tail hook comes from the hook on the back of fighter jets that is used to catch the planes when they land on an aircraft carrier.

it left, it took off at phenomenal speed. The next day a bunch of black sedans showed up on the base. Each one had four guys all dressed in black with hats. They got out and went to every building on the base and "encouraged" us not to talk about what we saw. I'm not easily intimidated. I know how to use a firearm and I've flown in combat conditions, but these guys meant business."

Colonel Rogers

Colonel Rogers had retired from the military and lived alone. Rogers had mentioned to some people he had seen UFOs and his work in the military had assured them that they were real. Several days later a man dressed in black showed up at his door. When Rogers opened it the man began to warn him about not talking about UFOs. Rogers told the man, "OK, just a minute." He excused himself went into his bedroom and came back to the front door with a loaded .45 pistol. He cocked it, pointed it at the man's head and said, "I don't know if you are CIA, NSA, or an alien, but somebody will have a lot of explaining to do if I blow your head off. Now get out of here."

The next day another man showed up wearing regular business attire (no black suit with shades). He hailed the colonel from the front yard with his arms raised, said he was unarmed, and asked if he could talk to him briefly. The colonel allowed the guy to approach. The guy said, "Look Colonel, we're sorry, no more guys will show up at your house. Some of this UFO information is still classified and we would appreciate it if you just didn't talk too much about it. OK? Thanks." And, then the guy left.

Black Helicopters

These are similar to the Men in Black. Abductees, contactees, and people who have UFO encounters often report being followed by black helicopters. Once again, no one is sure if these are government aircraft or alien craft disguised as helicopters. There are cases which point to both.

One contactee, author Kim Carlsberg, has recorded being followed by black helicopters on the days following a nighttime abduction experience.

Unconfirmed sources say these black helicopters belong to the U.S. Army's, 160th SOAR Division. The helicopters are black, or in some cases a very dark green, because they are "stealth aircraft" technology and cannot be detected by radar, just like the stealth bombers and fighters. Apparently these craft are also made available to other government agencies, including but not limited to the CIA, FEMA, and NSA.

FEMA

FEMA stands for the Federal Emergency Management Agency. This is the organization you hear about on your local news whenever there has been a hurricane, tornado, earthquake, flood, or any other major catastrophe. FEMA manages the funds that are doled out by the government to states and individuals to help them recover from these events.

In looking into covert or "black" operations, FEMA comes up again and again. It appears that FEMA is used as a cover to direct funds into these covert operations. However, FEMA turns up again and again from all kinds of different sources whenever government secrecy and funding is the topic. No other "civilian" agency does. Not only that, but after any major disaster people seem to have a hard time getting relief from this agency, as if there were not enough money there.

CHAPTER ELEVEN

UFO RETRIEVAL PROJECT

Sergeant Clifford Stone is a remarkable man and tells an amazing story about the history of UFO's and extraterrestrials dating back to the early 40's[40]. Sergeant Stone discusses with great familiarity the ending of Project Blue Book and the supposed interest of the U.S. Air Force in UFOs and what really happened. He also discusses the formation of the UFO Retrieval Project and the work it has performed over the decades as well as General Douglas MacArthur's involvement in the UFO mystery. When I met Sergeant Stone in Roswell he very kindly gave me a lot of documents that confirmed his story. Among them is the following information that he offered for my use.

---

[40] Clifford Stone tells this story in a fascinating book entitled "Eyes Only: The Story of Clifford Stone and UFO Crash Retrievals". Stone, Clifford, "Eyes Only: The Story of Clifford Stone and UFO Crash Retrievals", 2011.

General Douglas MacArthur organized a group called the Interplanetary Phenomena Research Unit back in 1943 to study this issue and the organization continues its mission to this day. Their purpose is to recover objects of unknown origin particularly those that are of non-Earthly origin. They obtain field intelligence information and pass it on to those who are the "keepers of this information."

Stone says that even Project Bluebook had an elite investigation unit, which was outside of Bluebook. This unit was thought to be working in conjunction with Bluebook but in fact was not. Stone has seen living and dead extraterrestrials in his official duties on an army team that retrieved crashed ET crafts. He thinks that the extraterrestrials will not permit us to explore the depths of outer space until we've learned to grow spiritually and that they will make themselves known soon if we don't first acknowledge their presence. On February 26th, 1942, commonly called the Battle of Los Angeles, witnesses report that there are some 15 to 20 unidentified craft flying over Los Angeles. Military Units immediately responded by trying to shoot these objects down. The 37th Coastal Artillery Group expended 1,430 rounds and witnesses report there appeared to be a number of direct hits. We immediately set out to try to find out if there was some hidden base belonging to the Axis from where these planes could come, some commercial airport that they could have had these aircraft housed. None of this bore out. Every search effort we made turned out to be fruitless.

At the same time in the Pacific the U.S. Military was experiencing the same phenomena, the so-called Foo Fighters. General MacArthur directed his intelligence people to find out what was going on. There is reason to believe that in 1943 MacArthur found out that in fact we had beings not of this Earth and visitors from some other planet visiting our planet that was actually observing that world event we call the Second World War. One of the problems that he had was that, should this be the case, and should they prove to be hostile, we knew very little about them and we had very little means to defend ourselves.

In response to this potential problem, MacArthur organized what was called the **Interplanetary Phenomena Research Unit**[41]. The organization would later be taken

---

[41] The Interplanetary Phenomenon Unit (or IPU) was a United States Army staff section established by at least 1947 and supposedly dissolved by the late 1950s.

Officials have confirmed that the IPU existed, but little else is known about it. It seems to have been an unidentified flying object-related undertaking. Some ufologists have suggested that the very name "Interplanetary Phenomenon Unit" is an indication that the IPU was convinced that the extraterrestrial hypothesis was a viable explanation for UFOs.

There has been speculation that the IPU was another name for the Majestic 12 or MJ-12, an unconfirmed (and controversial) U.S. UFO research group said to have been founded in 1947 to handle UFO investigations in the aftermath of the so-called Roswell UFO incident.

Another contention is that the IPU was a separate unit, also founded in 1947 following Roswell, under the direction of Army Counterintelligence, but ultimately at the disposal of MJ-12. Researchers William Steinman and Wendelle Stevens contended the IPU unit was directly involved in the crash-recovery of another UFO at Aztec, New Mexico in March 1948, being ordered there by MJ-12.

However, another MJ-12 related document of questionable authenticity, indicated the unit was supposedly established early in 1942 by General George Marshall following a well-publicized UFO incident, the so-called "West coast air raid" or "Battle of Los Angeles" in which an unidentified object or objects over Los Angeles resulted in a massive anti-aircraft barrage.

General Douglas MacArthur has also been rumored as involved in the formation of the IPU, during or towards the end of World War II, because of the many UFO incidents occurring under his command in the Pacific. Allegedly MacArthur reported directly to General Marshall.

Maybe supporting MacArthur's involvement is the fact that he did make public statements on at least three occasions that Earth might have to unite to fight a future war against an alien menace. Two such quotes were in the New York Times, October 8, 1955, and July 5, 1961. Another was a famous speech at West Point, May 12, 1962, in which he said, "We speak in strange terms: of harnessing the cosmic energy ...of ultimate conflict between a united human race and the sinister forces of some other planetary galaxy; of such dreams and fantasies as to make life the most exciting of all time." Wiki source The same quote also appeared in a July 4th speech MacArthur delivered in Manila in 1961.

In May 1984, William Steinman first wrote the Army Directorate of Counterintelligence, since, according to Steinman's information, the IPU was run out of the Scientific and Technical Branch of the Directorate. Steinman received the following reply from a Lieutenant Colonel Lance R. Cornine. Cornine claimed that the IPU had only an unofficial existence and refused to definitely acknowledge the existence of any unit records:

over by General Marshall, and in spite of what has been said about it disbanding, there is evidence that it has continued all the way through to present day. Names have been changed and records still haven't surfaced. The Army tries to state that it was not an official organizational effort to try to investigate UFO's. But it was organized by a General, it bore a fruit, it came to conclusions that were not

---

:"As you note in your letter, the so-called Interplanetary Phenomenon Unit (IPU) was disestablished and, as far as we are aware, all records, if any, were transferred to the Air Force in the late 1950's. The 'unit' was formed as an in-house project purely as an interest item for the Assistant Chief of Staff for Intelligence. It was never a 'unit' in the military sense, nor was it ever formally organized or reportable, it had no investigative function, mission or authority, and may not even have had any formal records at all. It is only through institutional memory that any recollection exists of this unit. We are therefore unable to answer your questions as to the exact purpose of the unit, exactly when it was disestablished, or who was in command. This last would not apply in any case, as no one was in 'command'. We have no records or documentation of any kind on this unit."

In March 1987, British UFO researcher Timothy Good also wrote the Army Directorate of Counterintelligence and again received a letter confirming the existence of the IPU from a Colonel William Guild. Guild was more definitive about the existence of IPU records and that they had been turned over to the U.S. Air Force Office of Special Investigations (AFOSI), the USAF counterintelligence unit, and the Air Force's Project Blue Book:

:"...the aforementioned Army unit was disestablished during the late 1950's and never reactivated. All records pertaining to this unit were surrendered to the U.S. Air Force Office of Special Investigations in conjunction with operation BLUEBOOK."

Good also stated that the IPU reported directly to General Marshall. Documents from AFOSI about the IPU, if they exist, have never been released.   http://wikibin.org/articles/interplanetary-phenomenon-unit.html

popular, i.e., interplanetary spacecraft were visiting this planet. And they continued to do exactly what they do today and that is to be part of a multi-intelligence operation in the recovery of objects of unknown origin particularly those that are of non-Earthly origin. Their purpose is to assess that information, get raw field intelligence data, and process that data into some type of useful intelligence product to disseminate to the field- to those people who have a need to know and those people that are, shall we say, the keepers of that information.

One of MacArthur's Air Force generals, an Army Air Corps General at the time, came back to MacArthur and told MacArthur "what we have is something not of this Earth". I would suggest that by this time even the Germans had uncovered evidence that we were being visited and had some type of physical evidence. MacArthur definitely had physical evidence. From the documentation I saw [while working this issue in the Army], I was not able to ascertain exactly what that physical evidence consisted of but it was there.

The one thing I find quite unique is that the Germans may have tried to back-engineer one of these objects. We definitely tried to back-engineer it. But we find that your technology has to be on par with the acquired technology in order to back-engineer it...

In the 1950's, the United States Air Force had an elite unit to investigate UFO's outside of Bluebook. Even though Bluebook felt that this unit was working with them, they were not. This unit was initially organized as a 4602nd Air Intelligence Service Squadron. Among its peacetime missions was operation Blue Fly. Operation Blue Fly was to recover objects of unknown origin that fell to Earth. It is very important that you remember these were specifically objects that fell to Earth- because we didn't have any spacecraft up there at this time. As a result of this, they had monitors right there at Wright Patterson that when UFO reports came in they were looked at very closely to see if there was any possible necessity of sending out teams to recover any of this fallen debris.

The Air Force states they never used them. I'm telling you I know they did. But the intent of the Operation Blue Fly peacetime project was to go out and recover objects of unknown origin that impacted with the Earth. Later it would be expanded in 1957 to cover all objects of unknown origin meaning spacecraft too. And it would become part of what they would call in the October of 1957 timeframe, Project Moon Dust.

Project Moon Dust is the overall field exploitation to recover only two items: First, objects of non-U.S. origin that survives re-entry into the Earth's atmosphere and impacts with the Earth and objects. Naturally, we would be interested in those items from a technical, scientific intelligence basis to determine, or try to ascertain the technical capabilities of any potential enemy since our known enemy of the U.S., the USSR at that time that was launching space vehicles into space.

The other area of interest was objects of unknown origin. Now we find that there were quite a few objects of unknown origin that did not correlate with any known space launches, impact times, or any known space debris falling back to Earth.

In short, under [Project] Moon Dust and under Blue Fly, we have recovered alien debris not of this Earth.

The degree of classification that we have now has changed over the years. Back during the time of the Second World War all the way up to, say 1969, you may have had as many as 11 classifications. Now there are three: confidential, secret and top-secret. However, if you have information that is highly sensitive that requires protection above and beyond the norm of what is provided for those classifications, that's when you have the Special Access

Programs. You do not get that type of information out into public domain unless it is officially sanctioned.

During the discussion of UFO's, the question ultimately is going to come up can any government keep secrets let alone the U.S. Government? And the answer to that is unequivocally yes. But one of the greatest weapons the intelligence community has at their disposal is a predisposition by the American people, the American politicians, and the debunkers- people who wish to try to debunk UFO information. They immediately come out and say oh we can't keep secrets, we can't keep secrets. Well, the truth is, yes we can.

The National Recognizance Office remained secret for many, many years. The mere existence of the NSA remained secret. The development of the atomic weapon remained secret until once you exploded one you eventually had to tell some people what was going on.

And we are conditioned by our own paradigms not to accept the possibility or probability of a highly advanced intelligent civilization coming here to visit us. You have evidence in the form of highly credible reports of objects being seen, of the entities inside these objects being seen. Yet, we look for a prosaic explanation and we throw out the bits and pieces of the evidence that doesn't meet our paradigm. So it is a self-keeping secret. You can conceal it in plain sight. It is political suicide to go and start hitting up intelligence agencies to get this information released. So most of your members of Congress, and I know I've worked with a lot of them along that line, will balk and try not to do it. I can name you three members of Congress that were point blank asked to have a congressional inquiry on what happened here at Roswell.

One of the most ridiculous statements that I got was that a person would have to be a chairperson to do that. So I asked a senator from Mississippi if he'd do it and without any hesitation, he said no. I said, would you give me that in writing? I got that in writing but I'm hesitant to release it. I will show it to you but I'm hesitant to release it simply because I made a promise not to.

We have got to get the documentation as it exists in the Government files. We have got to get it released before it ultimately is destroyed. A good example is the Blue Fly and Moon Dust files. I had classified documents the Air Force acknowledged. When I got members of Congress to help me open up more files they were immediately destroyed and I can prove this.

Somewhere along the line they may see that material and realize there is some very highly sensitive information that would have a damning effect upon the national security of United States should it become compromised. It needs to be further protected to insure that there is only a limited access to that information to a small number of people. So small you can put them on a list of paper, on a piece of paper, and list them by name. Thus you have the Special Access Programs. The controls that were supposed to be put on the Special Access Programs are not there. When Congress did their review of the way we protect documents and the way we go ahead and implement our secrecy programs they found that you had Special Access Programs within Special Access Programs -- that it was essentially impossible to keep control of them all by Congress. And I'm telling you right now; it is essentially impossible to keep control of them all.

When it comes to UFO's the same criteria applies. Therefore, only a small nucleus within the intelligence community numbering less than a hundred -- no, I'd suggest less than 50 -- control all that information. It is not subject to congressional review or oversight at all. So Congress needs to go ahead and ask the hard questions and convene a hearing.

There would be quite a few missions to describe but simply put, yes, I was involved in those types of operations to retrieve crashed ET objects. A lot of people think that you are just in your unit waiting in the rafters, just waiting for the next UFO crash, a landing where there is going to be debris. It doesn't work that way. You have a real life. You have a real job in the military. However, if you are in an area where an event takes place and you are one of these people that they can go ahead and call upon in your field of expertise, then you are called in.

Now, in order to prepare me for this, very early on in my career they sent me to NBC School at Fort McClellan, Alabama. It's a three-week school. It's for NBC personnel, NBC meaning Nuclear, Biological, and Chemical. And it would always be in the context of an NBC unit that I would be involved in UFO retrievals. You would go ahead and deploy as though it was a nuclear accident. There are procedures already established on nuclear or biological or chemical accidents. So you would proceed in that way. If you could get in there and do recoveries, if you could go in and extract the debris that are there quietly behind the scenes and no one knows, you'd do it. If you needed an officially sanctioned deception program to come into play, such as a bogus news release, you could do this also.

For example, if you have an airplane accident we have standard procedures on how we handle that. Those same procedures are utilized when you do a recovery or extraction of a crashed ET spacecraft or debris thereof. And I have to stress debris simply because these are highly advanced technical machines. There were not that many crashes. They are flawed because they are made by an intelligence that is as mortal as you or me. Being mortal, we are subject to error.

Now, we are talking about a highly intelligent civilization, not a highly incompetent civilization. We take steps and they take steps. But at the same time, when you go out, you make a recovery. And when you make that recovery, you handle it the same way you would as if you were out there on an airplane accident or you have a hazardous material type situation, because it works. It is all set up. The only problem you have is that you have people out there that are very quickly going to realize that this is not something of this planet. To be sure, with the Blue Fly recoveries [ET craft], you do what is called an on-site analysis.

In short, you have experts out there who know what missiles are, who know what aircraft are. They are looking at this material. They are telling you what it isn't. This leaves you to only one possible conclusion, something that did not originate on the face of this planet. That was the intent of the Blue Fly teams. It was very critical to do an immediate on-site analysis. Now, the way you package the material if it is just debris is handled the same way you would if it was hazardous material. You took precautions. If you had a whole craft, you took very serious precautions because while I still state the ET's are not hostile, you still could cause some serious accidents, which would result in death. I'm not going to get into how it was with the family when I had to leave on these operations because you get a little emotional because you think about what could happen...

Of course, you try to conceal the material, particularly if you have a large craft and it is disc shaped or say, wedge shape -- which is a very good shape that we get from time to time. And you take precautions particularly if you have to go ahead and put it on a truck to bring it in. If you have to put it on a truck to take it to a safe haven area, we track that truck. The truck has an 800 number so if there is a breakdown they can secure the vehicle and stay with it. But they have a number they can call and immediately get assistance out there to move that vehicle to a safe haven area. And there are procedures outlined in this. As a matter of fact, you have a shipping document. And that shipping document has the number right on it to call. So you use a code word -- I'll give you one that we used all the time: Tabasco.

In the case of an ET craft, you are going to get a specialized team out there that knows what to do should there be a biological component. One of the big concerns we had was biological due to contamination as a result of this being truly of alien origin.

I am prepared to state that I have been at locations where craft of unknown origin that did not originate on the face of this planet were there. I am prepared to state that while I was there, we saw living and dead bodies of entities that were not born on this planet. I am prepared to state that we had what they referred to as "interfacing" with those entities. I am prepared to state that they have a school to try to indoctrinate people. I never went to that school. I always refused. I am prepared to state that when I got out of the service in 1990, that they held me for two months so that I might better reconsider to stay in and not get out. I am prepared to state that I had orders that stated that I was supposed to get out on December 1st of 1989, and that they revoked those orders. Once again, in violation of law they held me for two months pending approval of my retirement, which had already been approved. The purpose of that was to try to convince me to stay in.

We have contact with aliens not originating from some foreign country but from some other solar system. And I have been a party to that. I've worked it. I've been there. And I know some of the things we do is really, really, really, really terrible. They are not hostile toward us. We are the enemy in this instance -- but we are the enemy, I like to think, for the good reasons. We are concerned about what some other country might do. I have concluded that I am fighting against the clock. That I have but a short time to try to convince people that we are moving down an avenue where we are going to militarize space. Once we militarize space we will have a whole new avenue of technology open up to us.

NASA says it is going to take another 1,400 years before we achieve what we call interstellar travel. I'm telling you by the end of this century we will be doing that. If we do nothing to grow spiritually -- and this is a hard thing for me to state -- but if we do nothing to grow spiritually we will not achieve interstellar travel. They will stop us. What's worse they will make themselves known to an unsuspecting people on this planet.

We want to acquire this technology. We want to make this technology part of our own technology. Within the next 25 years we are going to militarize space. As a result of militarizing space, we are going to acquire new technologies and we are going to evolve new technology that is going to lead us into interstellar travel. As a direct result, we will become a threat to them unless we spiritually grow also. But I feel that if we do not grow spiritually we are forcing the situation where the entities will eventually make themselves known. And they will make themselves known. And no power on Earth can stop that from happening. The ET's will do this in order to stop us from going out into space as a threat. If this should happen, it will happen to an unsuspecting world population and that can create some very serious problems.

But this doesn't deal just with the United States. It is a truth that the entire world has to be informed about. And that truth is that man is not alone, that we have people from other planets, from other solar systems coming here.

I believe that the intelligence community had good intentions when they classified information dealing with UFO's. I believe that they asked some very serious and hard questions: What impact would it have if the peoples of the world knew that they were no longer alone in the universe, that they had intelligence that was visiting this planet? And I think that the intentions were good there. As intelligence agencies among nations, naturally you want to go ahead and acquire the technology for military application. So you want to try to keep some of that knowledge as confidential as possible by classifying it as high as you possibly can- keeping the information open to only a small handful of people thus, Special Access Programs. However, I believe that while it was full of good intentions in keeping this information classified, it is [now] hurting people.

I do not believe that any government has the right to try to make individuals who merely see UFO's look crazy. I do not believe that any government has a right knowing that the psychology of specific individuals may ultimately lead to a tremendous amount of mental depression, ultimately, leading in many, many cases to suicide or self-destruction. When we see these types of things coming about, we have an obligation to reconsider our thoughts and positions. I would suggest [that] we need to break down the walls of secrecy, that we must be responsible in getting the truth out. We must be responsible in how we get that truth out. And we must be truthful.

And it is not a scary story. You will learn that the ET's have a perception of God. You find they have families. You find they have cultures. You find that they have likes and dislikes. You look for those things that are similar among us, not the differences. And that is the way you start on the path to truth. The problem that we have right now is that we look at them as something to talk about; something to marvel at and be amazed at.

Well, back to my own story, we had just finished the training that I took to be an NBC NCO. And a friend of mine brought me back to Fort Lee, Virginia. He was going to Fort Meade, Maryland and says, come on, I'll give you a ride to your base. And we discussed UFO's on the way to Fort Lee.

Several weeks after I got back to Fort Lee, I got a call from this person and I was going to visit him at Ft. Meade. When I got to Fort Meade where he was supposed to be, they said, well, he is going to be tied up we'll talk to you later about his situation as soon as he gets free. This person says, by the way, have you ever been to the Pentagon? Well, at that time I had never been at the Pentagon. So they said, well, it is really a unique place. Why don't we go ahead and give you the twenty-five cent tour. So we went on over. We went in. I had a little badge that was given to me, no picture on it. But the guy that was with me, his had a picture and he'd just tell the guards he is authorized to come with me. And he'd always be the one to get me in. Finally we got to a place that has an elevator. We went down on it- I don't know how far down we went. I can't tell you if there is one flight under the Pentagon, two, or fifty. But we went down. When we get out there, there are two monorails there. I mean, there are monorails under the Pentagon. They look like big tubes, rather thick in the center, one on each side. So you had these little monorails with cars that look like a bullet, where you could seat two people in front and two people in back. We got on the one monorail and started to go, it seemed like maybe 20 minutes, but I'm guessing at that because I don't know for sure.

When we got out, he says, well, let me show you some interesting sites down this corridor here. So we are going down the corridor and it looked like there was a door at the far end of that corridor. As we got closer and closer to that door, my guide turned to me and stated, you know, things aren't always as they seem to be. He says a lot of people don't know about these underground locations underneath the Pentagon. Only a few know that the Pentagon has underground monorails that connect up to other locations. He says, it is just like the walls here -- they don't all seem like walls. And I said, what do you mean they are not walls? I said, what are you talking about? I thought, you know, he was trying to make a joke. At that time he says, no, it is like the wall behind you. I look and it looks like a wall to me. There are no seams or anything I can see. Then he pushes me. I try to grab myself but there is actually a door that opened.

Well, when you go through the door there is like a field table there. And behind the field table you had this little entity. The entity was a little bigger than the 3, 3 1/2 foot tall entities that are a lot of times reported. But there were two men on either side of the table slightly behind the creature. When I turned around, I looked right into the eyes of this little creature. And you know, it's like you are seeing it but everything is being pulled from your mind-he was reading my whole life. It is hard to describe what I really felt there- your life up to that point goes by in seconds. And I mean you were feeling everything.

I remember going down and grabbing a hold of my head like this and falling to the floor. The next thing I remember I wake up and I am back in my friend's office [back at Fort Meade]. And when I'm back in Jack's office they told me nothing happened that I had been there the whole day. But I knew better.

I will go this far to state that there is an interaction between entities and certain Government agencies within the U.S. Government. I will not go so far to state that they are giving us technologies to kill ourselves. They are not along that line. Their purpose in being here is for scientific purposes and for humanitarian purposes.

We have been very foolish in how we have done certain things and we have harmed ourselves. We now realize that we have harmed ourselves and we are trying to take corrective action. And that right there is the one thing that the ET's are checking on. There is the biosphere that's been damaged. They are not coming here to repair that. They are coming here to see how we handle it. But a government can't be the one that shoulders all of the responsibility and shoulders all the knowledge and all the understanding. The whole situation is that we have to work in unison as a people, a united people. We must go ahead and start preparing ourselves to where we ultimately will take that giant step to where we are going to be visiting other planets out there in other solar systems. And we have to, once again, I'll use the word, grow spiritually as a group of people, the people representing mankind on planet Earth.

Yes there is some type- and I don't know to what extent- but there is some type of dialogue that is taking place between our visitors of all species, because there is more than one, and the various governments- not just the U.S. Government, but of the worlds. Primarily, these are the more developed nations of the world because at present space faring nations represent the greatest threat to them.

Another early experience I had was an accidental viewing of something I was not supposed to see. We were in a facility and a friend and I went to a balcony area looking down over the briefing room. They had a Plexiglas window that separated the balcony and what was going on downstairs- you couldn't hear what was being said. But we started to notice that they were running a film. And the film showed various types of what we would call UFO's, today. It showed various types of alien creatures some that looked very much like us some that looked like us with marked differences. We were not aware of the fact that there were people now up there with us. And they said, what are you guys doing up here? And we told them, well you know we are just sitting up here eating our snacks because we didn't want to go to the snack bar. They said, you need to come with us and you need to come with us now. So I mean they pushed us grabbing us by the nape, the shirt, and pushed us down the stairs.

Once they got down the stairs, they pushed us on out the doors and into a van. The van was right there waiting, a panel van, where they pushed us in and shut the door. And then they drove us off. We don't know where they took us to but the location where we finally got out was a one-frame military style building. They took us in there, put us into this room. The room had the military cots there. It had one table with a light. And we were sitting back trying to figure out why are they doing this? Why is this going on?

On the fifth night, I got out and they drove me back to my billets. I reported in and went to bed because I was dead tired and all I wanted to do was get some sleep. The next morning, which was a Saturday morning, I am awakened by the CQ, that is, Charge of Quarters. And he says, I want to see you. Well, I was taken to see two men; one guy was acting like a good guy. The other guy went ahead and said, I told you we shouldn't trust him. Let's just take the so and so out. Let's just end this. Let's shoot him. And the nicer guy says, no, no, we'll discuss this. And he sent the guy that was supposed to be the bad guy out- we use that technique sometimes in security- good cop, bad cop. The one that was supposed to be the bad guy, he went to get some food.

The good guy says, listen, he says, you like working with this UFO stuff. And I'm saying, no, I don't. And he says, well, you know, you have experience with it. You've had some involvement. He says, and those were not phony pictures up there. He says, would you like to work with it? Would you like to work with us? I said, no I wouldn't like that at all. Eventually he goes ahead and says, look, you like working with, you'll get to work with it, you'll get to learn more about it, he says. He says the whole situation is that by the end of this year we are going to release everything we know. But here again the world is not a safe place. We have to know more from a technological viewpoint and a military standpoint than potential enemies of this country know. So I'm asking you -- work with us. Well, I thought about it. And you know, I was young. And I thought this is something that I've actually been involved with all my life, that it'd be fun, that I could go ahead learn certain things, answers to the questions I had, actually get a better understanding of events in my life.

I do believe that, one, they wanted me in the military; two, they wanted me involved in this program; three, there wasn't really concern about, if at some later date, I started to talk about it. They were only concerned what I might have to prove: If I had some little slivers of proof, what impact would that have on my story. But I know they did not want me out of the military. I know they wanted me to stay in. I know they wanted me to go ahead and go to what they referred to as The School. But I would never commit myself to go to what they were referring to as The School.

I was told that if you go to the school it will open up a whole new world for you, a whole new avenue. But I had to agree to it. And I had to go ahead and sign specific papers to go to it. And I was not prepared to go to that school. I had seen people who were involved with the program that had gone to that school and let me just say I didn't like their personality. I did not like the idea that by you going there it made you something special, it made you a prima donna, if you wish. That was not the way it was supposed to be. I felt that one of the greatest things you can be is a servant and not vice versa.

So some of these people, I did not like their disposition. I did not like their attitudes. And I did not want to become like them. And one of my fears was if I went to the school it would change me the same way.

Now, there are events, there are recoveries [of ET craft]. But the recoveries are few and far between. One of the events that took place in 1969 was a recovery of a craft that was a wedge shape craft and took place in Indian Town Gap. Now, I know it was cold and I believe it to have been in the winter but there was no snow. We were on a field training exercise, the 96th Civil Affairs Group. I was part of the 96th Civil Affairs Company. I was the NBC Non-Commissioned Officer in Charge. We were notified that they had an incident involving a downed craft and we needed to assist in recovery. The persons that showed up knew exactly where we were going and we went to our staging area. From there we went to another location in Indian Town Gap. We didn't have any problems about civilians or curiosity seekers or anything like this. The situation is, we did the recovery. I realized that what I was seeing was not of human origin.

When we got there, there was already a team set up. Floodlights were always set up around the object. I was asked to get closer and closer to the object to take readings with the APD 27. As I did this, I realized what I was seeing was not of an Earthly origin. I'm hesitant to go into it too much, because I don't want to get emotional about it...

Bentwaters is another very interesting case. With Bentwaters, we went there to digest some of the information. As far as the physical evidence, there were photographs. There was film footage. There was evidence of a higher than normal background radiation. Not all that high, but above normal. We found that there were some abnormalities in the area we referred to as the impact point. We also noticed that the trees had been leveled off at the top. When we got there, it was late December, I want to say December 28th was the day that we arrived there.

We gathered up the materials. We took these materials back to Lindsey Air Force Base, all the hard evidence that we could get, all the documentation that was there. There were sightings that were picked up on radar. Both the British Government and the U.S. Government were aware of these sightings. The hard evidence that we had was taken back to Lindsey Air Force Base. There it was digested to where there was some type of information that could be put out to brief Shape Headquarters [NATO]. And I don't know who in Shape Headquarters was briefed. But I do know that we did have to do that. The information was then put with the special courier. I believe it was coming back to an air base close to the Washington, D.C. area and that the materials transferred on to Fort Belvoir,

Virginia, headquarters at the time of the U.S. Air Forces
Special Field Activities Group, Air Forces Field Activities
Center. They then took this material, did whatever they did
with it, and came up with the finalized intelligence product.

The reason it went to Lindsey was because the U.S.
Air Forces Field Activities Center had detachments in the
field. The closest detachment in the field to Bentwaters
would have been Lindsey Air Force Base. They were the
ones that got the material. They were the ones that were
charged with safeguarding it until it got back to the U.S.
They were asking questions, hard questions, critical
questions. They were asking technical questions of
technical people that were involved. I know for a fact that
some of the radar operators, both British and U.S. were
questioned. I know some of the people were out there on
two different nights and they were questioned.

I was also involved with the Belgian UFO events in
June, July of 1989. We were assessing information,
gathering data on the UFO over flights of Belgium. The
UFOs also went all over Germany. We had one incident
there on the border near the Soviet territory. We saw that
the Soviets were pretty upset because this was a huge
object. It was triangular shape about three football fields on
either side of the triangle. It flew over what we call No-

Man's Zone. As it flew over there we all were getting jittery.

It was, I'd say summer, about August. You could feel your hair standing up on end. It was more than just, you know, getting shivers because of fright or something like this. There was some type of physiological effect taking place. Once this incident subsided, we put fighters on alert. We notified them that we may have a Soviet craft coming across the gap and we were going to intercept it. The Soviets did the same thing. It went back over the Soviet airspace and they scrambled fighters to try to intercept it. It wasn't traveling fast at all. But on this particular night no one fired at it.

There were pictures taken. There was consultation with the Soviet Union. With this going on, everyone was taken in and briefed. People were informed that what they saw was nothing more than a Russian MIG 27 that had strayed across into the area far enough into the No-Man's Zone to create a problem and cause some alarm. But it was no MIG 27. We knew exactly what we were looking at. You have flashcards which are silhouettes of the various craft of the Soviet Union and even our own.

So we knew precisely what we were looking at. What we saw was a craft that was of an unusual origin. It was not aerodynamically sound. And when I state it was not aerodynamically sound, I mean it had no means of staying aloft like that without some visible means of aerial support like a helicopter. That wasn't there. It was perfectly silent not making any noise roughly three stories high. This was one of the incidents that got me a little concerned, made me think about wanting to get out and come back to the family, to have some family life. We had the incident escalate. We had it escalate to where the Soviet Union filed an official protest through the Belgium Government to the U.S. Government stating that they were very concerned about the Belgium authorities along with several other countries letting us fly stealth aircraft on reconnaissance missions into the Soviet Union. We notified and discussed it with the Soviet Union. We briefed at least the Soviet Military Liaison Mission Groups that this had nothing to do with our involvement of sending stealth aircraft into their territory.

The Soviet Union was alarmed about what was going on. They even alluded to it being our craft. They were reassured that it wasn't. We reassured the Belgium authorities that it wasn't. The Belgium authorities had their own UFO sightings. We have seen this on TV. What you don't know about those sightings is that there was a tremendous- I don't want to call it a cover-up- there was a movement to keep specific information about those sightings under wraps. There were some efforts to go ahead and alter the film footage of the radar screens to the point where it showed the UFO going underground, which it did not. I think it was supposed to have gone 600 feet into the Earth. That did not happen. It was visible. People saw it. The pilots saw it. The pilot's aircraft locked on to it. But these were things that would create more questions that we were willing to answer. So we decided to keep this out of the press. And we were successful at it.

Another case we were involved with was the Iranian incident of September 19th, 1976. Both fighters were taken apart to try to find out if there was any way we could explain what really happened to those fighters which were having malfunctions at the same time. There was a situation where we had some anomalies picked up out where the sighting was- where one of the Air Force pilots saw the UFO go down to the ground. We recorded those anomalies with audio devices. We took film footage of the area and there were some strange things that showed up on that film footage. Everything that took place there at the landing area, I am not privy to. I don't have all the information. It wasn't something I had to be involved in. But I can tell you this much, whatever took place there had people out there for two to three weeks.

In 1986, I believe it was, we fired at a UFO on two occasions. The UFO took off like nothing happened. In '86 you had the incident where you had 20 or more UFO's flying around Brazilian aircraft, flying rings around them. These documents are important.

Not more than two-dozen UFOs had been retrieved by 1969 when I was briefed first. We were informed that there had only been a couple dozen tops- that there were several in the '40's and the early 50's. And to make it perfectly clear about those events that took place then, it sounds crazy but our radar wreaked havoc on the ET guidance systems and they had to make adjustments to their guidance systems for that.

How many bodies had been recovered? Don't know. How many crashes have occurred in which we only got debris because the ET's came and did their recovery before we got there? Don't know but it has happened. It has happened. When they had problems, just like we send out a distress call, they send out a distress call, which is something that a lot of people don't think about; it's a question that's never asked. But here again we think of them as something intangible like that stuffed animal there.

But they are living, breathing creatures as mortal as you and me. They think, they have loves, they have likes, they have dislikes, in short, they have social culture.

This is so important to try to make people understand that that is the case. I want to put the human factor back into UFO's. And when I say the human factor, I mean that these are real people. You can call them entities. You can call them creatures. But you sometimes find yourself wondering: who are the more real people, them or us? And these are things that really need to be brought out-the fact that they are just like you and me. We need to seek out the similarities, not the differences and come to a greater understanding. Because eventually, in the not too distant future, we are going to have that final contact that is going to open new doors...

A lot of people sit back and say, well, they don't have bases here. Ah, yeah, they do.

We were involved in a major engagement in 1970 in one of their bases in Vietnam approximately seven miles from the Cambodian border. If you want to know more about that, I did an audiotape on that. And I'll make you a copy of the audiotape. I will apologize for actually trying to hold back from some of the stories simply because if I start talking about some of the stories you start reliving them.

APPENDIX ONE

OTHER CRASHES

- 1897-The Aurora, Texas UFO Crash

Occurring during the "Great Airship" wave of the late 1800s, the legend of a UFO crash and a dead alien has survived over a century of debate. Allegedly, the dead alien pilot is buried in the local cemetery. The story of the crash was related by local newspapers, the UPI, and AP. The city received "historical site" status because of the incident.

- 1941-The Missouri UFO Crash Retrieval

Brought to public knowledge by UFO investigator Leo Stringfield, from an account by Charlette Mann. Mann related the story of her grandfather Reverend William Huffman, who claimed to have been called to the scene of a crashed UFO with dead aliens outside of town.

- 1947-The Roswell, New Mexico UFO Crash

The most famous UFO case of all occurred near Corona, Mexico. Rancher Mac Brazel found strange crash debris on his morning rounds, and reported his find to local radio station. Soon, the military from Roswell AFB was involved, and issued a press statement that the Air Force had captured a UFO.

- 1948-UFO Crash at Aztec, New Mexico

Author Frank Scully described the Aztec crash as that of a craft which was measured at exactly 99.99 feet in diameter, covered by a material which resembled a light weight, shiny metal that possessed incredible strength and durability. It seems that nothing on this earth could penetrate or damage the hull of this craft from another world.

- 1953-UFO Crash in Arizona

The eyewitness was working for a company that had a government contract at a nuclear site in Nevada. He was summoned by his boss on 5-21-53, and sent on a "secret" assignment. Arriving at their secret destination, two military light-alls illuminated a surreal scene in the late night, pre-dawn skies of the desert. The engineer was amazed to see a disc-shaped craft embedded in the sand.

- 1965-The Kecksburg, Pennsylvania Crash

On December 5, 1965, something came from the skies of Canada, Michigan, Ohio, and Pennsylvania, finally crashing into the woods near the town of Kecksburg. Frances Kalp was the closest to the crash, and reported it to the local radio station. Soon, Pennsylvania state police and U.S. military took over the investigation.

- 1967-UFO Crash at Shag Harbor, Nova Scotia

Eyewitnesses see several unknown objects in the sky, and soon they crash into the seas of Shag Harbor. Rescue workers, fearing a plane crash, rush to the area, only to find bright, yellow foam on the ocean. Several days of search find nothing. Investigators believe the object, still intact has left the area.

- BATTLE OF LOS ANGELES 1942

Summary:

It is very rare that among the annals of Ufology there should appear a UFO case which involved military, yet is accompanied with actual photographic proof. Such is the case of an event which took place over the Los Angeles area on February 25, 1942. A giant UFO would actually hover over the city, and be witnessed by hundreds of observers.

Pearl Harbor Scare:

As America was gathering its senses after the shocking attack on Pearl Harbor in December, 1941, there was a heightened feeling of insecurity and anxiousness. The skies were being watched as never before as a giant UFO moved through California, alerting the military and civilian watchers as well. This case is known as the "Battle of Los Angeles," and is one of the most important cases in Ufology.

Surreal Sight:

It would be early morning on February 2, 1942 when the incoming craft sirens were first heard in the Los Angeles area. Many Americans were expecting another wave of Japanese fighter planes, and thought this is what they would see as they left their homes, and ventured outside. How wrong they were! The first sightings of a large UFO would be made in Culver City, and Santa Monica.

A Total Blackout:

Air Raid Wardens were ready to go at the first hint of an invasion. But, this invasion would be something other than Japanese planes. The giant hovering object was soon lit up by the gigantic spotlights of the Army's 37th Coast Artillery Brigade. Everyone who looked up was shocked by the sight of the giant UFO sitting above their city. Military aircraft were sent to confront the object.

UFO Takes Direct Hits:

Because of a well-organized alert system, the whole California southern section was searching the night skies in a matter of minutes. What they saw were beaming searchlights illuminating the night sky, all of them converging on one thing-a UFO. A similar scene would be repeated later during the Norwood Searchlight Incident albeit, on a smaller scale. The beams of light would soon be accompanied by tracer fire from anti-aircraft artillery, all of the rounds aiming at the invading craft. The giant UFO would take direct hit after hit, yet without damage.

Hanging Magic Lantern:

The 37th Brigade was relentless in its attempt to bring down the large object, but found no success. The barrage of spent shells would fall over the entire area-no place was safe this night. Many were injured, and there were even reports of death from the falling shells. According to newspaper reports, eyewitnesses described the sight of the UFO like a "surreal, hanging, magic lantern."

Classic Photograph Taken:

As the large UFO moved into more lighted areas, view of the object became better. It moved directly over the MGM studios in Culver City. Fortunately, an extremely good quality photograph was taken of the object-beams attached, tracer fire visible. This photograph has become a classic UFO photograph. The UFO would soon move over Long Beach before disappearing altogether.

Woman Air Raid Warden Gives Testimony:

Woman Air Raid Warden Gives Testimony: "It was huge! It was just enormous! And it was practically right over my house. I had never seen anything like it in my life!" she said.

"It was just hovering there in the sky and hardly moving at all. It was a lovely pale orange and about the most beautiful thing you've ever seen. I could see it perfectly because it was very close. It was big!"

More Eyewitness Testimony:

"They sent fighter planes up and I watched them in groups approach it and then turn away. There were shooting at it but it didn't seem to matter."

"It was like the Fourth of July but much louder. They were firing like crazy but they couldn't touch it."

"I'll never forget what a magnificent sight it was. Just marvelous. And what a gorgeous color!" she said

The Guns Fall Silent:

The giant invading airship was now gone, and the citizenry of the southern California area began to resume normal activities. This was an extremely important event- one that will not be forgotten.

Only the news of the war kept this from becoming a major news event. This case must have been in the mind of President Ronald Reagan when he warned us of an "alien threat, from outside of our world."

INDEX

1

160th SOAR Division, 169

3

37th Coastal Artillery Group, 172

4

4602nd Air Intelligence Service
    Squadron, 177

5

509th Bomb Group, 18, 28
509th Composite Group. *See*
    509th Bombing Group
5th Bomber Command, 36

8

8th Air Force, 26, 27

9

96th Civil Affairs Company, 197

A

**Air & Space/Smithsonian
    Magazine**, 32
Air Force Office of Atomic Energy
    (AFOAT-1), 37

Anderson, Gerald, 115, 117, 118, 119
Angel of Death, 4
Apodaca, Eddie, 133, 137
Archuleta, Valentin, 97
Armijo's' old Horse Springs store, 120
Aztec, New Mexico, 95, 174, 206, 213

B

Baca, Harold, 115, 116, 123
Baca, Remigio, 126, 129, 137
Ballard Funeral Home, 23
Barnett, Barney, 115, 116, 118, 122, 123
Battle of Los Angeles, 172, 174, 208
Bell UH-1 Huey, 87
Bender, Albert K., 161
Bentwaters, 197, 198
Berliner, Don, 11, 118
Berlitz, Charles, 116
Bermuda Triangle, 79
Biggs Field, 88, 91
Black helicopters, 112, 169
Blanchard, Colonel, 22, 25, 26, 31, 32
Blanchard, William Col., 20
Bosque del Apache National
    Wildlife Refuge, 124, 135
Brazel, 16, 17, 18, 20, 28, 29, 30, 31, 37, 42, 47, 155, 206
Brazel, W.W. "Mack", 16
Bush, Vannevar Dr., 56, 109

C

Cahill, Helen, 50
Cape Girardeau, Missouri, 148, 212
Cashon, Charles A., Maj., 27
Cavitt, Sheridan Capt., 20
Combat Photo Interpreter/ Intelligence Officer, 36
Corona, 10, 11, 28, 29, 118, 122, 144, 155, 206
Corona, New Mexico, 10, 155
Coyame, 73, 74, 75, 80, 81, 82, 84, 89, 90
Crash At Corona, 11

D

Danzer, Roy, 51
Dave Farr, 117
Dennis, Glenn, 23, 49
DuBose, Thomas Brig. Gen., 27
Dugger, Barbara, 49
Dwyer, Dan, 51
Dwyer, Sally, 51

E

Egyptian pyramids, 79
El Paso Oil Company, 101

F

FEMA, 169, 170
Ferguson, Bill, 101
Fisk, Walter Wayne, 153
Foo Fighters, 173
Fort Bliss, Texas, 4, 82, 87, 88
Fort Worth Army Air Field. See Carswell Air Force Base
Fort-Worth Star Telegram, 43
Fowler, Raymond, 53, 54, 61
Freeman, George P. Colonel, 163
Frenchman's Flat, 70

Friedman, Stanton, 39, 96, 118, 153
Fronabarger, Garland D., 150

G

GeBauer, Leo, 110
Golubic, Victor, 118

H

Hart Canyon, 101, 108
Haut, Walter, Lt., 25, 34
Hopkins, Herbert Dr., 160
Horse Springs. See Magdalena
Huffman, Guy, 153
Huffman, Reverend William, 148, 205

I

Interplanetary Phenomena Research Unit, 172, 173
Interplanetary Phenomenon Unit, 109, 173, 174

J

Johnson, Bond, 42, 43
Johnson, Bond Colonel, 43

K

Kingman UFO retrieval, 53, 54
Kirtland Air Force Base, 98
Kralyevich, Vincent, 90
Kuznik, Frank, 32

L

La Zona del Silencio. See Zone of Silence
Lincoln County, 10

M

MacArthur, General Douglas, 171
Magdalena, 46, 114, 115, 116,
  117, 119, 121, 123, 129, 144,
  212
Mann, Charlotte, 147, 149, 150,
  153, 154
Marcel Jr., Jesse, 18, 21, 22, 30, 35
Marcel, Jesse, 35, 36, 38
Marcel, Jesse Antoine, 35
Marcel, Jesse Maj., 18
Marcel, Major, 20, 21, 22, 26, 30,
  36, 42
Marfa Army Airfield, 91
Marshall, General, 174, 175
Men in Black, 157, 159, 160, 164,
  169
Mexican Roswell, 73
Miller, Scott, 90
Moffett, Ben. *See* Mountain mail
Moore, William, 116
Mountain Mail, 119, 129, 137
MUFON, 44, 91

N

National Recognizance Office, 179
NBC School, 182
Noland, Doug, 101, 102, 105

O

Omega Press, 3
Operation Blue Fly, 177
Oppenheimer, Robert Dr., 109
Owl Café, 124, 140

P

Padilla, Faustino, 127, 133, 142
Padilla, Jose, 126, 128, 137
Payne, Bud, 28

Plains of San Agustin. *See*
  Magdalena
Press release, 25, 27, 28, 32, 33,
  139
Proctors, 17
Project Blue Book, 163, 171, 175
Project Moon Dust, 177

R

Red Star Baptist Church, 148
Roberts, Judd, 28
Roger M. Ramey, Brig. Gen., 26
Roswell, 10
Roswell Army Air Field, 18, 30
Roswell Army Airfield Morgue, 24
Roswell Daily Record, 25, 27, 28
Roswell UFO Museum, 14, 22
Rowe, Frankie, 50

S

San Agustin Plains, 114, 116, 117,
  121, 122
San Antonio, New Mexico, 124
Sandoval, Manuel, 96
Schade, Clarence R., 153
Schauberger, Victor, 56
Scully, Frank, 100, 101, 106, 107,
  108, 206
Shape Headquarters, 198
Shirkey, Robert Lt., 25
Sikorsky CH-53D, 87
Space Review. *See* Albert K.
  Bender
Stancil, Arthur G.. *See* Fritz
  Werner
Steinman, William, 108, 174
Stevens, Wendelle, 110, 111, 174
Stone, Sergeant Clifford, 171
Strategic Air Command, 37
Strickland, Lyman, 28
Stringfield, Leonard, 57, 90

T

Texas
    El Paso, 3, 4, 5
The Associated Press, 25
The School, 195

U

UFO Retrieval Project, 171
Uhouse, Bill, 57

V

Van Neuman, John, 111

W

Wang, Eric Dr., 54, 55, 63, 68

Wang. Connie, 4
Watkins, John Dr., 21
Werner, Fritz, 54, 55, 61, 62, 68, 69
Western Union telegram, 45
Whitmore, Walt, 28
Wilcox, George Sheriff, 18, 49
Wilcox, Inez, 49
Woody, William, 19
Wright-Patterson Air Force Base, 54, 55

Z

Zamora, Lonnie, 127, 143, 144
Zone of Silence, 77, 79

CPSIA information can be obtained
at www.ICGtesting.com
Printed in the USA
FFOW03n1754271217
44166902-43552FF

9 781933 951911